STRIPPED

Learning to Live and Love After Rape

Brenda M. Gonzalez

Copyright © 2017 by Brenda M. Gonzalez

All Rights Reserved

Published by Author Academy Elite
P.O. Box 43, Powell, OH 43035
www.AuthorAcademyElite.com

Printed in the United States of America

All rights reserved. No part of this publication may be reproduced, stored in a retrieval system or transmitted in any form or by any means – for example, electronic, photocopy, recording – without the prior written permission of the publisher. The only exception is brief quotations in printed reviews.

Library of Congress Cataloging-in-Publication Data

Gonzalez, Brenda M., 1975 –

STRIPPED: Learning to Live and Love After Rape

ISBN: 978-1-64085-058-3 (pbck)
ISBN: 978-1-64085-059-0 (hback)
ISBN: 978-1-64085-060-6 (ebook)

LCCN: 2017909166

To protect the privacy of ancillary characters in this story, some names have been changed.

The internet addresses, email addresses and phone numbers in this book are accurate at the time of publication. They are provided as a resource. AAE Publishing does not endorse them or vouch for their content or permanence.

To my family and friends who have lived with and loved me through this, I wouldn't have made it this far without you. Thank you.

*Good friends help you find important things
when you have lost them...
Your Smile
Your Hope
Your Courage*

~Doe Zantamata

Contents

Introduction   1

Part 1: Surviving

Let's Begin	7
Making Friends	11
Don't Talk to Strangers	13
The Morning After	17
The Longest Commute Ever	23
Pause for a Caveat	28
Homecoming	30
The FBI – Just Like on TV (or not)!	33
Reality Blows	36

Part 2: Learning

The Diagnosis – PTSD	43
Voodoo Witch Magic (AKA Somatic Experiencing)	56
PTSD: My New "Normal"	59
Tips For Managing a Panic Attack	61
The "R" Word	63
Guilt is a Bitch	67
Trust Issues	69
Anger	72
Work in Progress	74
The Pursuit of Happiness	80

Part 3: Living

Journal Entry: Introduction	91
Journal Entry: The Darkness	92
Journal Entry: Creativity	93
Journal Entry: The Power of Touch	94
Journal Entry: Can't	96
Journal Entry: The Water Taxi	97
Journal Entry: My Mom	99
Journal Entry: Questions	100
Journal Entry: Walking with Jesus	101
Journal Entry: The Presence of Fear	104
Journal Entry: Medicated	105
Journal Entry: Change	106
Journal Entry: God is Good	107
Journal Entry: When?	108
Journal Entry: 25 Days of Zen	110
Journal Entry: Reassurance About Writing this Book	116
Journal Entry: More Voodoo Magic	117
Journal Entry: Reiki? Yes, Please!	118
Journal Entry: Wish	119
Journal Entry: More Voodoo Witch Magic	120
Journal Entry: Meditation	122
Journal Entry: Optimism	123

Part 4: Loving

A Real-Life Nightmare – a husband's story	127
How to Hire a Hitman – a best friend's story	152
Wait…Mom was Raped? – a daughter's story	159
Knowing Brenda – a college roommate's story	162
"My Brenda" – a mother's story	177

Part 5: Rejoicing

A Victory Dance   187

Part 6: Knowing

Tips for Traveling Safer   193
Other Useful Tips You May or May Not Know   195
Tips for Survivors   197
National Resources for Survivors   199

Acknowledgements   201
Epilogue   203
Notes   205

At the end of the day, all you need is hope and strength. Hope that it will get better and strength to hold on until it does.

~Lupytha Hermin

Introduction

I remember the day I was raped like it was yesterday. I can tell you exactly what I did that day. I know what I was wearing down to the color of my socks, and I can even tell you what I had for dinner that evening. One of my most vivid memories, though, was vowing not to tell a soul. I was ashamed. I was embarrassed. I knew it was my fault.

If you picked up this book, it's likely because sexual assault has touched you in some way, shape, or form. Either you were raped recently or as a child, or you love and care for somebody who was raped. Statistics show that 1 in 6 women will be the victim/survivor of sexual assault in their lifetime. Stop and think about that. 1 in 6 women. How many women do you know? Now do the math. If we talked about rape and sexual assault like we do cancer or divorce, it would be a topic you'd see posted about on Facebook and discussed over coffee. But it's not. It's shameful. It's taboo. It's rarely talked about.

In this book, you'll learn I eventually told my husband, a few family members, and a few close friends. I couldn't survive the aftermath alone. I, like you, was looking for support. But more so, I was looking for answers. I wanted to read about somebody else's experience. I wanted to know what I was feeling was normal. I was desperate for information. Unsurprisingly, there are not many books out there from the perspective of the victim, let alone the people who loved them through it.

As I pondered this fact, I realized I needed to tell my story in order to heal. When I did begin opening up and talking about it, the feedback was astounding. People started telling me about their own experiences, or that of their grandmother, daughter, sister, aunt, or roommate. There was this connection like, "I get it, sister. I know."

This book is written for every rape survivor and all the people who love them. The body heals, but the memories aren't forgotten. For years, I've had more bad days than good. I'm working on that. I want to get to the other side, where the good days surpass the bad. I'm alive — that's a pretty good start. I know what's important in my life. I know how resilient I am. Most importantly, I know I am loved and never have to face the day alone.

In my obsession with self-help books, I've collected a myriad of quotes, one of my favorite being from Mira Kirshenbaum's *Everything Happens for a Reason*. "What you need is a better story of yourself. Your old story had to do with how afraid you were. Your new story will have to do with how resilient you are." That's the truth I'm living by now.

This book doesn't have all the answers. It simply has my story, my feelings about living in the aftermath, and the unique perspective of the people who are loving me through this. There is no happy ending. I'm not "cured," and I still have days where I don't want to take a shower or get out of bed, but if you have those days — know you're not alone. There's a sisterhood (and brotherhood) of survivors out there, and you don't have to look far to find them. Check out my notes in the appendix, I'll provide a list of resources at your disposal.

I hope this book helps answer some of your questions and normalize some of your feelings. If you want to join me

INTRODUCTION

in my journey, follow me on Facebook at Brenda G Author or contact me via email at BrendaGAuthor@gmail.com.

Peace and Love,
Brenda

Part 1: Surviving

Brenda's Story

There is solace in breaking our silence. A strength of spirit when sharing our truth. It all starts with the choice to live on the other side of victim.

~ Christine Macdonald

Author's Note: This section contains a very graphic depiction of my rape. This could be triggering for you. If you think it may be, please join us in Part 2: Learning. You'll be caught up in no time.

Let's Begin

I was wearing gym shoes that day.
Running shoes, to be specific. The irony of it all?
I couldn't run that night.

I had nowhere to run, no one to run to, and I had no idea who or where I was running from. All I knew was I was naked. I was afraid. I was in danger. And, unlike on TV shows, nobody was coming to rescue me. I was on my own.

I had been in Sochi, Russia for a week. I was working for a Worldwide Olympic Sponsor, and it was my job to scope out the advertising locations we would purchase during the 2014 Winter Games. The process, like most things in Sochi, was unclear and unorganized. The only way to determine the path forward was to go check it out in person.

The first hurdle was getting to Sochi. The visa process is arduous, even with the resources of one of the largest advertising agencies in the world. In terms of transportation, there is no easy route to Sochi. My colleague, Lynn, and I boarded a plane in Chicago, flew to London, and then headed to Moscow. We met up with my counterpart, Ivan, at our sister agency. We did some preparatory work, and a few days later, the three of us boarded the flight to Sochi.

I'd been to Sochi once before, but my clients had been with me. When you travel to foreign countries with clients, their local office usually arranges things such as security, drivers, hotels, etc. We didn't have the luxury of traveling with clients this trip, and we were on a strict ad agency budget. Not quite the same. Ivan had arranged transportation with a driver who, unfortunately, didn't speak much English. We were fine the first part of the week when Ivan was with us to translate, but things went downhill after he left.

We arrived in Sochi after dark. It was September 2013, so preparations for the Games were in full swing. Everything was under construction, and I mean *everything*. Once we found our driver, we headed to the hotel. The roads were all under construction. Buildings were under construction. The Olympic Park was under construction. Even the entrance to the hotel was under construction.

The driver couldn't figure out how to get us to our hotel because of the construction. It was a problem that took more than an hour to solve. He eventually cut through a construction site, drove over large stone piles, through dirt paths, and wrapped around several fences I'm pretty sure said "Do Not Enter" (in Russian) until he was able to deliver us to the vicinity of the hotel. Close enough.

It was late when we arrived, and the hotel was quite full, as it was one of the few hotels open in Sochi and in close proximity to the Olympic Park. Lynn was assigned to a smoking room on the 7th floor. I scored a non-smoking room on the 2nd floor. After doing the obligatory paperwork, registering our passports, reviewing billing, etc. we finally settled into our rooms. My room was lovely. New construction, large, clean bathroom, king size bed, flat screen TV...I was happy to have finally arrived.

The next day, Ivan, Lynn, and I attended a meeting for Olympic sponsors to review the media planning process. As expected, the meeting was conducted in Russian. Even being there in person, with a Russian representative, proved how disorganized the process was going to be. Ivan and I spent the afternoon reviewing paperwork and trying to figure out

PART 1: SURVIVING

a way to make the client happy. The opportunities being presented were nowhere comparable to what had been accomplished during the London Olympics in 2012. It was going to be a challenge. The next few days were spent driving around Sochi, looking at their advertising spaces and feeling defeated. We couldn't find the "wow" factor we were looking for, and we weren't delivering news the clients wanted to hear.

By Thursday night, everything was falling apart. The Chicago advertising team had presented the ad campaign without my knowledge and without the context of where the ads would be running. When the CEO asked for specifics on the media placement, the advertising team didn't have the answers to give him because I hadn't found the answers yet. It was going to take the limited amount of time I had on the ground to figure out what, exactly, my response would be. I hate not having answers, and I hate it even more when people are speaking for me. My frustration was mounting.

The next day was somewhat successful. We found solutions that had not been offered in the Olympic advertising options presented at the meeting earlier that week. Ivan and I felt optimistic. We excitedly called the client from the car to tell him what we had found. His response was not met with the enthusiasm we'd anticipated. He told us the campaign was pretty much dead at that point, but he'd give us one more shot at reviving it.

We took that challenge and told him we'd have a full-blown recommendation by the start of business the next day. We ended our day feeling relieved. Ivan headed back to Moscow. Lynn and I stayed in Sochi and developed a plan. We worked at a frantic pace to have a presentation prepared to share as soon as the client was ready to hear us out. We were going to save the day. The downside? Time. 5PM Friday Chicago time was the earliest he could carve out time for us.

Ummm…that was 2AM in Sochi.

Did he really think we were going to do a conference call at 2AM? Yes. Yes, he did. Swear words ensued after we hung up the phone. We ate sushi at the hotel and then we waited. And waited. And waited. Lynn and I did the conference call from the king size bed in my hotel room, in our pajamas, so tired we could barely form words. We presented the plan. It was brilliant. I was confident we could sell it and save the day. However, the client was cranky because it was the end of the day on a Friday (SERIOUSLY!?!! It was 2 o'clock in the damn morning in Sochi!) He thought the ideas were good, just wasn't sure they were good enough to take back to the CEO, as he had already said no to the campaign. We hung up the phone at 2:18 AM, exhausted and defeated.

This trip officially sucked.

Making Friends

Saturday morning, Lynn and I decided not to work. We slept in, had a leisurely brunch, and I even went to the gym for a run. We decided to have our driver take us up to the mountain area of the Olympic Park, where the sledding and skiing events were to be held. It was raining, but it was still beautiful. We took the gondolas even higher up the mountain. We had an amazing dinner at a hotel on the promenade.

After a week of pure suckiness, we were actually enjoying ourselves. When we got back to our hotel, we headed to the hotel bar to do a shot of Russian vodka. It was our version of "when in Rome." We threw back our shots, ordered two beers, and were having a good time reminiscing about the time we had spent together in London. The Olympics really do bring people together.

The bar grew a little busier. Lynn went to the bathroom, and I heard a woman a couple of seats down saying she needed more girlfriends. Being my usual friendly self, I invited her to hang out with Lynn and me. The boisterous, foul-mouth group of guys accompanying her invited themselves to hang out with us too. When Lynn got back, I had a group of new friends to introduce to her. She laughed. We had just been texting a friend we had made in London at a local pub back in 2012. What can I say? I'm a people person.

We found out this motley crew was comprised primarily of Brits, specifically electricians and riggers for the opening and closing ceremonies. The best part? THEY SPOKE ENGLISH!!! Over the course of the evening, we learned about UK Geography and drew maps of the U.S. to test our own geography skills. (For the record, I am very good.)

Kerry, our new female friend, had the most beautiful auburn hair. Larry was an older gent in his late fifties. He had worked on the Olympics in Beijing, Vancouver, London, and now Sochi. He thought this would be his last Games. It was a tough lifestyle, and he had been having some health problems. There was a younger guy, blond, chipped front tooth. Ironically, he was Larry's boss, which is the perfect example of not judging a book by its cover. I don't remember his name, but he left with a somewhat unattractive woman. Later, he explained he had made a bet with the guys — 3,000 rubles if he slept with the ugliest girl in the bar. They all thought she was a lesbian but he "won" the bet (even though I'm guessing he convinced her to go along with the story for a portion of the winnings).

Then there was Mark — he was very tall, thin, and muscular. He threw his money around, talking trash about his wealthy family back home. He liked me. He tried to kiss me at one point and flat out asked me to go back to his hotel room. Taken aback, I politely declined, pointing out that I was married, and informed him the only person I was leaving the bar with was Lynn. He seemed okay with it. He continued to flirt but didn't make me particularly uncomfortable.

There were a few more guys around us. Lynn was talking to one of the quieter ones sitting on her other side. I didn't catch his name. Larry made me laugh because he said he was surprised we were so much fun. He thought we'd be stuck-up American girls — too good to hang around with the lot of them. Then somebody bought a round of tequila shots, and everything went black.

Don't Talk to Strangers

The next thing I remember is "coming to." The best way to describe it is like waking up from anesthesia. My body felt paralyzed. There was a man on top of me. He was having sex with me. It made no sense. I was so confused. Who was this guy? Why couldn't I see him? Why was everything so blurry? He moved me where he wanted me. I couldn't fight back. I couldn't find my words. I was so thirsty. I needed water.

There were three sexual acts I remember. They're hazy, but I have shameful memories of them. He didn't talk much. Although at one point when he was on top of me, he was speaking to me in a different language. All I could say was "I don't understand what you're saying" but my mouth was so dry, I don't know if the words actually came out.

I think he was speaking Russian but every now and then he'd say something in English. Either way, I couldn't comprehend. I was in and out of consciousness. I tried to open my eyes, but they wouldn't open. Everything he did to me was rough. If he was holding my leg, he would dig his fingers into my flesh. If he was kissing me, he was biting my lips until they bled. If he was moving me into a different position, he was tossing me around like a rag doll. After what seemed like forever, I was in a position of being able to roll off the bed and land on my knees. I thought I would be able to pull myself up into a standing position. It didn't quite work as planned, but I was able to crawl to the couch, close to the bed, and bring myself up to a sitting position. He said nothing. Thankfully, he just sat back and watched me struggle.

I knew I had to get myself out of the room. He seemed annoyed that I was awake but didn't say anything. He just watched me from the bed. I managed to stand up and get myself into the bathroom. I remember him telling me not to close the door, which was fine because that would have required coordination I didn't have. I went to the bathroom, still unable to see or focus on much. It hurt to pee and, from what I could tell, there was blood.

I went to wash my hands and splash water on my face/eyes trying to get my vision back. When I looked in the mirror, there was more blood. It was primarily by my left eye, my nose, and there was a lot of blood in my mouth/on my lips. I could taste it. I could smell it. I wanted to vomit. My hair was matted and full of knots. There was blood on the strands by my face and sticky stuff (I assumed was semen) plastering my hair in weird directions. I didn't recognize the girl in the mirror. I pitied her.

A strange calmness took over. I was certain this shell of a body was going to die. I had no voice. I could barely see, and I had no control over most of my limbs. I stumbled out of the bathroom and found my clothes. Awkwardly, and with no emotion, I started to get dressed. Again, he didn't say anything, just stared at me. Oddly, the clothes were perfectly folded in the order he took them off with my shoes untied and laid on top of my clothes, upside down so they wouldn't get my clothes dirty. He didn't even unhook my bra to take it off — he slipped my sweatshirt, t-shirt, and bra all over my head at the same time. They were all folded nicely together.

PART 1: SURVIVING

My jeans were folded along with my underwear, neatly set on top. They were all sitting perfectly on his desk chair.

Getting dressed took a lot of effort. My entire body ached. Putting on my jeans was the WORST. I couldn't tie my shoes. For the first time, I realized my hands were numb. I remember hitting my forehead on his desk when I leaned over in an attempt to secure them to my feet. I had no sense of balance and again, really couldn't see what I was doing. He said nothing, he just stared at me.

My purse was sitting on his desk. I wanted to text my husband Henry that I was in trouble, but my phone was missing. My passport and what little jewelry I had been wearing were in there, though. I started asking the stranger questions like, "I don't remember how I ended up in your room, do you know?" He'd say no. I said, "I'm really confused." He'd say he was too. I said, "This isn't like me. I don't do one night stands." He said neither did he.

I asked if he knew where my phone was — he said no. I told him I needed to find it — that maybe I'd left it at the bar. It was my excuse to leave the room. He said he needed to walk me there because the overnight bartenders only spoke Russian. He put his pocket knife in his pants. He walked me to the bar, told me to look down and not say anything, and to let him do the talking. They spoke in Russian. The bartender did not have my phone. He then asked what my room number was. I told him I was fine to walk myself to my room and he said no, he was going to walk me back to my room.

I assume he didn't want me going for help or for the security footage to show me stumbling all over the place, or worse yet, passing out in a hallway. He walked me to my room, standing behind me, holding my left shoulder and right hip. Much too close for my comfort. The whole time I was sure he was going to slit my throat from behind. I made it to my room, but I was hesitant to open the door because

I was afraid he would force his way in and the nightmare would start all over again, or that's where he would dump my body after he killed me. But he only kissed/bit me one last time and walked away.

I remember thinking *What the hell just happened? Does this guy know how bad he hurt me? Why did he let me go? Do I say 'thank you' (for not killing me?)* The confusion was unbearable. I got myself into my room, found my iPad, and texted Henry that I thought I had been drugged, I didn't have my phone, and I was feeling unsettled but that I was safe in my room. It was 4:30AM. I didn't even take off my shoes before I passed out again.

The Morning After

The next morning was, by far, worse than what I remember about the rape. My body had cold sweats, I couldn't open my eyes without my stomach rolling, and I drank both bottles of water from the mini-bar within minutes because I felt so dehydrated. Dried blood was still caked on my face and remnants were left on my pillow.

I had to pee, but the pain was excruciating. I took off my jeans when I was in the bathroom and saw I had softball size bruises on the top and insides of my knees. Finger marks on my calves. Huge bruises on my thighs. I finally got brave enough to check the girl parts; I had bruises where no girl should ever have bruises. I didn't even know you could bruise like that down there.

As the day went on, more and more bruises appeared. My right wrist. My right bicep. Fingerprints on my throat and on the tops of my breasts. My nipples had been bitten; one had dried blood on it. I still couldn't open my left eye. My face hurt. My nose hurt. My forehead hurt. My chin hurt so bad, I couldn't let myself cry because the quiver of it nearly sent me through the roof. Even something as simple as wearing my necklace hurt my sternum. All I could do was sleep.

I eventually woke up and texted Lynn from my iPad that I had lost my phone. She said it was in her purse, which made no sense to either of us. In hindsight, I believe the guy put it in there so I wouldn't have it to call for help. I didn't tell her what happened. I told her I needed to sleep some more. The shakes and the nausea were overwhelming. I was out of bottled water in my room and drinking from the tap would only cause more problems I was sure my stomach couldn't handle.

The crazy thing about all of this is that my body was in shambles, yet I couldn't allow myself to believe I had been raped. This was my fault. I needed to pull myself together. I'd made a bad decision, gotten myself into a bad situation, and ended up having sex with some random guy who I couldn't pick from a lineup if I tried. I'd never had a one-night stand in my life. I'm not a prude by any means, but I do have extremely high moral standards about who I let touch my body. A stranger I met in a bar would not be on the approved list. How could I wrap my head around this and how in the world was I going to explain this to Henry? I was horrified, ashamed, and embarrassed. All the while, Henry was blowing up my iPad with texts.

> Was I awake?
> He was worried.
> Was I okay?
> He was worried.
> What happened?
> He was worried.
> Where's my phone?
> He was worried.
> Why was I not texting back?
> He was worried.
> Text him back.
> For God's sake, text him back.

PART 1: SURVIVING

He was overwhelming me, so I sent short answers and told him I needed to sleep some more. I'd text when I woke up again. I told him I was alive and safely locked in my room. That seemed like a good start.

I couldn't see out of my left eye, there were still crusty pieces of dried blood, and I did not have the words or the energy to text him. I certainly wasn't going to call him — partly because it hurt my face to talk and partly because there were no words to tell him what had happened.

Nobody would believe I had been raped. I had been in a hotel bar drinking with strangers. I had been working the room, making friends with everybody, and having a good time. I had been laughing. From the parts of the night I remember, the video surveillance would show me having a grand ol' time.

None of this made sense. Something bad had happened to me, but I couldn't process it. Who did I leave the bar with? I would not have left with a guy, and even if I had tried, Lynn surely would have stopped me. Who was that guy I was having sex with and why was I so beat up? It took a few hours to really wrap my head around the fact that this had not been consensual. I replayed what I did know:

> Fact: I woke up in some man's room, and he was having sex with me while I was passed out.
> Fact: The last thing I remember was doing a shot of tequila.
> Fact: I don't pass out from drinking — it actually gives me insomnia.
> Fact: Even as messed up as everything was last night, he didn't kill me. He let me go back to my room. Why? And did he know what he did to me was wrong?

Fact: When I went to get dressed, my clothes had been perfectly folded. Okay, so not an act of passion and I certainly didn't fold them. I don't even fold clean clothes at home.

Fact: The bruises on the top inside of my knees couldn't be from falling because the bruises would have been on the lower part of my knees. I was forcibly held down. The bruises are what convinced me all of this was real.

Fact: This was not consensual sex. I wanted to curl up and die. I was so ashamed.

I was 38 years old, and I had been raped. Drunk college girls get raped. Business executives working on the Olympics don't get raped. It simply made no sense. I couldn't comprehend. I couldn't process. I couldn't stop blaming myself. I was going to break Henry's heart. How could I have done this to him? I needed to pretend like it never happened. Bumps and bruises would heal. I would put this behind me, and I would be fine. I was always fine. I'd been through a lot in my life, and I always landed on my feet. This too was going to have to pass.

I attempted to clean myself up and eventually met Lynn downstairs at the hotel restaurant for lunch. She said I looked horrible. She asked if I had fallen. I told her I couldn't remember. I was too nauseous to eat, but there was water. I ran into Kerry (the woman from the bar) and an Italian guy who was also at the bar the night before. They asked if I was okay. I said yes. At that point, I didn't trust anybody.

All I wanted was to hide in my room and sleep. I didn't know what my attacker looked like. I didn't know if it was one man or five. I didn't know if there were photos or videos. I tried asking Lynn a few questions but her recollection from the night was vague too. Maybe she had been drugged as

PART 1: SURVIVING

well? Maybe she had been raped and was too ashamed to say anything to me? We talked about my visible injuries, with her trying to piece together a story to explain how I could have scratched my eye and hit the bottom of my chin. I tried to glean details of what could have happened after my memory failed me. Her memory wasn't great either.

What time did we leave the bar? 10:30ish.

Was I really drunk? She didn't think so.

Did I leave with anybody? Just her. There was one other guy on the elevator with us who got off on my floor, but she couldn't remember who it was.

I couldn't bring myself to tell her what actually happened. I was simply too ashamed and, in hindsight, too shocked. The fact that I had been in this man's possession for six hours explained the amount of damage my body had incurred. I was a smart, savvy, strong woman. How did I manage to get myself into such a predicament? There are no words to describe the guilt and embarrassment I felt inside.

She switched topics and decided we needed to update our presentation to include ideas we had come up with from our mountain visit. I bought myself a couple of hours to rest and then agreed to meet her in the lobby. I had trouble typing the presentation because my hands were shaking so badly. I had made a makeshift bandage to cover my eye using tissues and band aids. I wore my sunglasses over it, but I knew I wasn't hiding much. We did our work, I skipped dinner, and then I went back to sleep.

Henry's relentless texting added to the chaos already wreaking havoc in my head. Eventually, I told him I had been raped via text. Shock does funny things to your decision-making skills. I mean, who texts that to their husband?

I also sent a message to my best friend, Kelly. She has always been my voice of reason. While Henry was busy trying to figure out how to catch the man/men that did this to me, I knew I could count on Kelly to focus on me. She googled my injuries, sent recommendations on how to take care of my eye, and answered a few questions that were too personal to even write about in this book. I also emailed a few of my closest friends about what happened. I wasn't ready to talk about it yet, but I needed them to know. It made me feel a little less alone when I was halfway across the world — hurt and afraid.

I didn't sleep much on Sunday night. Once the sun had set, a new kind of fear kicked in. He knew what room I was in. What if he came back? I hadn't even showered from the night before because there was just no energy and I was afraid the water hitting my body would be devastatingly painful. I kept shaking. I needed more water to drink. I called room service but, of course, they didn't speak English. The rape didn't kill me, but I was going to die from dehydration.

The Longest Commute Ever

The next 72 hours were equally as horrible. On Monday, Lynn and I had to meet with the Olympic Organizing Committee to hash out a big problem we were having with our client's transportation services for The Games. At that point, I had to tell Lynn what happened because I needed her to step up and run the meeting. I explained I wasn't in the proper state of mind to represent our clients. She was in shock. She cried. My eye was still too damaged to produce my own tears, but I appreciated hers. We gently hugged in the back of the car. Like everything else in Sochi, the meeting did not go well, but they did have bottled water!

Once we got to the airport, the driver that had driven us around all week informed us, in very broken English and hand gestures, that he didn't take credit cards, only cash. That was problematic because it was over $1000 USD for the full week. Working in advertising, neither Lynn nor I had that kind of cash on us or in our checking accounts.

The driver, clearly irritated, wouldn't let Lynn out of the car, so I had to go into the airport by myself, clear the first security line, find an ATM machine (of course it was all in Russian), only to be denied because it exceeded the daily withdrawal limit and would overdraw my account. I called the bank to transfer funds from my savings to my checking and to inquire about increasing my withdrawal limit.

Between still being in shock, the noise in the airport, and a bad cell connection, I couldn't pass the security questions, and they wouldn't release my funds. I called back to try again. Denied again. I don't exactly know what happened next, but I vaguely remember sitting on the floor in the middle of the airport, screaming and crying at the customer service rep explaining I'd been raped and my co-worker was being held captive by a cab driver halfway around the world. I was begging her for help. I'm certain she thought I was nuts and passersbys had to think I was a crazy American. It only took 45 minutes to sort out, but it felt like hours. I was mentally and physically exhausted. But the day was only going to get worse.

After rescuing Lynn and clearing security, we were informed that our flight to Moscow had been delayed for two hours. The Sochi airport is small, our terminal was dirty, and it had very uncomfortable chairs. Every part of my body ached. I still couldn't see out of my left eye, and I felt like I had been hit by a truck.

Eventually, our flight was ready to depart, and we were able to escape Sochi. We landed in Moscow that evening to a torrential downpour and a parking lot that wasn't covered. I had my laptop bag, my carry-on bag, and my big, heavy suitcase to manage with a body that was bruised and battered. The driver helped Lynn carry her suitcase. I could have cried. *I* was the one that needed help! They were walking briskly in the rain while I could barely walk. I wanted to collapse in the parking lot. I wanted to scream. Instead, I slowly hobbled, did my best to manage the physical and emotional luggage I was carrying and made it to the car.

Traffic was worse than Chicago's Eisenhower Expressway on a Friday night. It was bumper to bumper to bumper. Every pothole was a reminder of how sore my girl parts were.

PART 1: SURVIVING

The seat belt crossing my sternum/collarbone was a constant reminder of my bruises and the mess I had created for myself. I was still only using one eye, wearing my makeshift eye patch. I was certain I was going to vomit — either from carsickness, being in shock, or my body trying to expel the drugs that may have still been in my system.

We finally arrived at the hotel in Moscow three hours after we landed. It was then I realized there had been a miscommunication between us and the local office regarding what time the car was scheduled to pick us up (3PM) vs. the time it was supposed to pick us up (3AM) to get us back to the airport to catch our flight into London. I stayed up another two hours trying to figure out how to get us to the airport. It was already after 11PM, but I was getting out of Russia come hell or high water.

While I prayed that my contact in the Moscow office was still awake and would see my email, I opted to finally shower. The ping of each drop of water sent pain shooting across every part of my body, but I could also feel the warm water washing off days of filth, the remnants of that disgusting man and the nastiness of the Sochi airport. I washed my hair over and over and over again, never feeling that it was clean enough.

The tears were there, but they still wouldn't come.

I'll never forget standing in the bathroom of the Ritz Carlton, on its pristine marble floors looking into a large, well-lit mirror and seeing my naked body in its entirety for the first time since it had been violated. It had been my body for 38 years but, for the first time in my life, I no longer recognized it. The fingerprint bruises covering it were not mine. The bite marks belonged to someone I did not know. The small bald patch of missing hair was not an accident. My swollen shut eye stung as I tried to open it. I *had* to be on that flight to London. I *had* to get home to Chicago.

As if on cue, my phone rang and my heart leapt. Maybe my Moscow contact had seen my email. Maybe the car would arrive, and I'd finally be heading back to the familiarity of Heathrow and eventually make it back to Chicago. I checked the caller ID. It was my college roommate, Kim. I looked at the phone like it was a foreign object. Was I ready to talk to another human? I had only communicated with her over carefully crafted emails, sounding braver than I felt, assuring her I was okay, though I was far from okay.

I hadn't talked to anyone besides Lynn and Henry up until that point. I answered, cautiously, not sure if I could form the words I wanted to say. I clicked ACCEPT and on the other end was the kindest, gentlest voice I'd ever heard. She was calling to check on me. Finally, for the first time, I cried. Big, ugly tears ran down my face, and I would have given anything not to have been alone in Moscow that night. My friends were still on the other side of the world, helpless to help me. I just wanted to go home.

The car situation worked out enough that Lynn and I made it to the Moscow airport, and of course, experienced another flight delay. Had I been capable of experiencing any type of emotion, landing in London would have been a joyous occasion. I was back in an industrialized nation, where people spoke English and showed less obvious disdain for Americans.

As we trekked across the airport, we ran into a glitch at security. For some reason, the metal detector beeped as I tried to pass into the international terminal. This required a full body pat down. While it had happened before, nothing compared to the pain of a pat down after the abuse my body had survived. It was indescribable, the shakes and sweats were uncontrollable. At that point, I was shocked I wasn't detained for further questioning. I was physically a mess. I could only guess what the TSA agents thought about me.

PART 1: SURVIVING

Lynn had also been flagged by security for having a water bottle in her bag. She was moved to another security line, so I found a nice, cool floor-to-ceiling post to rest my face on as I waited for her. A lovely security woman asked if I was unwell. I wanted to tell her my story, I wanted a doctor to fix my eye and give me something stronger than Advil for the pain, I wanted a magic ship to get me home without having to sit on another airplane for six more hours…but there was no way I was missing my flight. I. Just. Wanted. To. Get. Home. I told that lovely security woman I was fine.

After yet another lengthy delay, we finally boarded the plane headed towards Chicago. I had removed my eye patch, as my eye was used to being permanently closed by that point and the patch wasn't particularly comfortable. I settled into my First-Class seat, and for the first time, I relaxed. The only thing standing between Henry and me was the Atlantic Ocean and a U.S. Customs line. I was on a Boeing 777, so the Atlantic Ocean wasn't going to be a problem. The U.S. Customs line went about as well as every other part of the trip. The good news was they eventually let me back into the country.

Pause for a Caveat

Now, let's be clear. I know what you're supposed to do when you're raped. Don't take a shower, call the authorities, seek medical attention, etc.

However, we were in Sochi. Look at a map. We were closer to the Turkish border than we were to Moscow. There is no world-class hospital. Nobody speaks English. The chance of catching a disease at a medical facility there was higher than catching a disease from my rapist.

The other question, regarding law enforcement, is a joke. I am a U.S. citizen, visiting the Olympic Park on behalf of a Worldwide Olympic Sponsor, accusing somebody that I can't identify of slipping something into my drink, kidnapping me, and then raping me. That's not exactly the type of story Russia was going to let get out.

When a woman comes forward in the U.S., questions are asked about her state of mind, what she was wearing, how much she had to drink, did she really say no or was she changing her story. It's called victim shaming. It's horrible, and it's wrong and, of course, all of those things went through my mind.

Additionally, I was in a foreign country where people don't particularly care for Americans. I had a thorough education from Ivan the week before my trip about the corruption of local law enforcement. Bribes were expected if we wanted to place the ads where we were planning, and they would be

PART 1: SURVIVING

done with a handshake contract and a cash advance wired to a local businessman. Not exactly how I was used to doing business. In short, I was afraid it would be easier for local law enforcement to quietly make me disappear than deal with the PR nightmare my story would bring to their beloved country. Waiting until I returned home was my only option.

Homecoming

After clearing customs, my heart started to beat faster. I frantically looked around for Henry. He was coming to pick me up. No more strangers or car service for this girl, I was going to find solace in the arms of the man I love. Seeing his face and feeling his gentle embrace was enough to bring me to tears. Lots of tears. My body was still shaking like crazy, but I was home. I wasn't alone anymore. People were going to help me.

I had survived a rape 6,000 miles from home and managed to tackle each challenge of the 96 hours it took to get back to Chicago. Henry, on the other hand, was dealing with his own emotions. Helplessness. Anger. Frustration. Sadness. Fear. He was ready to fly to Sochi and find the monster that did this to me himself, but visa requirements wouldn't allow that. He tried calling the hotel to speak with security, only to find out they don't speak English there. He had wanted me to take legal action after I awoke from the drugs the next morning, but I was too afraid for the reasons noted earlier.

While he was trying to find answers as to how it had happened and to find the person(s) responsible, I had a singular mission: to get home. He had been in contact with our city's police department, who had put him in contact with an FBI agent that the officer knew, who had been in contact with the US State Department, who had been in contact with the Embassy in Moscow, who had been in contact with the

PART 1: SURVIVING

hotel. The only thing he was able to find out was that the hotel reviewed the security footage and didn't see anything that would have indicated I had been the victim of a heinous crime. Of course not.

Henry and I drove in silence from the airport to the community hospital in Geneva where a team of female doctors and nurses were awaiting my arrival. There was no check-in or triage, I was simply put into a wheelchair and whooshed quickly into a treatment room. The doctors and nurses were lovely — always explaining what was going to happen next, asking for my permission to touch me, looking over my body to document the bruises.

It had been 96 hours since the rape...too much time had passed to do a rape kit. It was my decision, though, if I still wanted one. I passed. I was much more concerned with my eye. An angel came into the treatment room and examined it. It was a scratched cornea. She gently held my eye open and rubbed a magic potion across it. My eyes watered. I'm not sure if it was because somebody was touching my eyeball, because I was finally able to open it after four days, or if they were simply tears, but I don't remember ever feeling as relieved as I did at that moment. I was home. Henry was sitting at my side, holding my hand, and this wonderful woman had given me my sight back. It was one less thing on my body that hurt.

They had to treat me for all STDs. I took 11 pills and received two shots. I couldn't get enough water, but they continued to bring me refills without me even asking. I wanted every toxin inside my body to be flushed out. There were x-rays, a rape advocate, and a call from the FBI. I did NOT want to talk to them. They offered to visit me at home the next day. Fine. There were warm blankets and a turkey sandwich. There was a whirlwind of activity around me, but I was safe. I was with Henry. I was home.

After we left the hospital, I had to face another reality — kids. Mine were 11 and 9 at the time and boy were they going to be excited to see me. It was Tuesday. I wasn't supposed to be home until Friday. I had been gone for ten days. It was going to quite the reunion. The problem? I was still battered and bruised. I explained they had to be gentle with me and told them a made-up story of my travel woes — sitting in coach, in a middle seat, next to a man who smelled, all the way home from London. They laughed, they sympathized, and they gave me long, gentle hugs.

The doorbell rang and there on my front step was Kelly with tears running down her cheeks. She had driven an hour and a half to give me a hug. We cried together and talked about how I would manage to explain this to my Aunt Susan, who was the closest thing I had to a mother, and whether I should tell my brother, Jason. We were orphaned as teenagers and held an unexplainable bond. But he was a recovering drug addict, and I didn't want him to use this as an excuse to relapse. I'd have to kick his ass, and I just didn't have the energy to deal with it. We decided we didn't have to decide that day. She didn't stay long, but I wanted her to stay forever. When she left, I put on comfy PJs and stayed as close as humanly possible to Henry for the rest of the night. My bed had never felt so good.

The FBI – Just Like on TV (or not)!

Thanks to Henry's overambitious desire to catch the bastard who did this to me, I consented to an interview with the FBI. They scheduled it to take place in the comfort of my home, during the day, so the kids would be at school. I heard the knock on the front door. As I tried to gather my composure, Henry ran upstairs to tell me they were driving white SUVs and had flashed their badges, just like they did on TV (though he did think the SUVs would be black). They were pleasant enough. Patient. There was a male and female agent. We went through my story in painstaking detail.

There were so many things about that night I couldn't remember. How much did you have to drink? I'm not sure. Were you drunk? I don't think so. Can you tell us what the man looked like? I don't know. How did you end up in his room? I have no idea. We were getting nowhere fast. They searched through my phone, read through my texts, looked at all of my pictures, checked my social media accounts, and read through my private messages.

If anyone ever wonders why rape victims don't go to the police after being raped, this is why. It's like being violated all over again. Interrogated. Looking for holes in the story. Trying to find pieces of the story or memories you may have missed or overtly left out. They collected the clothes I had worn that night and informed me they would need to have an FBI agent take "official" photos of my injuries. They would send another agent over later, accompanied by a female to ensure I was comfortable.

What. A. Joke.

The photographer and female agent came to my house closer to 5:00 when the kids were home from school. Henry needed to take them out so they wouldn't know what was happening. This made me incredibly uncomfortable. I didn't want to be home alone at all and certainly not with strangers. But I consented and Henry took the kids out to run errands. I was dressed in shorts and a tank top — showing enough of my body for the photographer to catalog photos of my bruises without having to remove clothes.

The photographer was, without a doubt, the most awkward man I had ever met. He was excited to be using the special equipment they use to document bodily injuries. He couldn't get the lens to focus though because my "skin was so pale!" Thanks, buddy, glad you noticed the lack of Vitamin D I've been getting.

Once he figured out how to get the lens to focus, the female agent held a ruler to document the size while he zoomed in on my bruises. We started at the bottom and worked our way to the top. I skipped over the most personal parts because I was now on day five, my private parts were healing nicely enough, and I simply didn't want to experience the humiliation.

As he photographed my body, he told me about the last time he did a photo shoot like this one; a friend of his had been kidnapped in Mexico and beaten with a machete. His injuries were worse, "Obviously." That's cool. Thanks for sharing and thank God, I had "only" been raped and

PART 1: SURVIVING

not beaten with a machete. I had never been happier to see somebody leave my house in my life.

A few months passed, and I eventually got the call I knew was coming all along. I was sitting in the parking lot of one of my favorite drive-thru restaurants. I had gotten a hot dog, cheese fries, and a Coke. My phone rang, and my heart sank. I knew it was the FBI thanks to caller ID, but it wasn't the agent I usually spoke with — this guy was an asshole. In short, because they couldn't get copies of the security footage from the hotel, because I couldn't identify my attacker, because I was "too drunk" to recall any details, because there was no DNA, "there was no evidence of a crime, and the FBI was closing my case." I hung up and sobbed. I couldn't even choke down my cheese fries. I love cheese fries.

Reality Blows

Once the euphoria of being home wore off, real life started to creep in. My work email was blowing up. I couldn't focus. I couldn't keep up. I emailed my boss and HR to explain what happened. For the record, there's no good way to word an email like that. They were shocked. I asked for 96 hours to "heal up" and then told them I'd be back at it. Little did I know, it would take me three months to get back to the office.

They told me to take my time. They had dinners sent to my house for a week, so I didn't have to worry about cooking. Everybody at the agency was informed that I was on leave and they weren't allowed to contact me. HR put me in contact with our Employee Assistance Program in case Henry or I wanted counseling. There was never a push for me to come back, just emails and phone calls to check on me. They handled the situation with extreme kindness and grace.

I took them up on the offer of counseling. That seemed like a good idea. A few sessions with a therapist to process all of this would get me back into shape in no time. They referred me to one of the women I credit with saving my life — Kimberly Rhodes. I came home on a Tuesday. I was in to see Kimberly the following week. Looking back, I was still in shock when I first walked into her office, but it would quickly become my safe place. A place where somebody

PART 1: SURVIVING

could explain all the feelings I had. I was a highly motivated, successful, type-A personality before Russia happened. Now I felt like a pathetic shell of a human being with little desire to participate in the real world. How was I ever going to get back to my former self?

The rest of that first week home is still a blur. I didn't have much of an appetite but eventually found solace in McDonald's Mighty Wings. Now, I'm not going to lie, I had never had Mighty Wings in my life prior to being raped, but we were going through the McDonald's drive-thru to get a coffee before a doctor's appointment, and at that moment, it struck me that I was hungry. I needed something with flavor. What little I had consumed up to that point had been bland. Mighty Wings sounded like they'd fit the bill. It was the best food I'd ever tasted in my life. For the next few weeks, I sustained myself with Mighty Wings and ice cream.

The next big challenge of being home was telling my loved ones what had happened to me. I had texted Henry and emailed my friends, but opted to tell my Aunt Susan, who's like my mom, and my brother Jason in person.

Kelly met me at my Aunt Susan's house because I wasn't sure I'd be able to say the words "I was raped" out loud. Kelly didn't want to say them either, but that's what Kelly does. She's my backup. With my best friend's arm around me, I told my Aunt Susan what had happened. She was speechless. We cried. We (gently) hugged. She asked a million questions I didn't have answers to. Kelly and I had a little bit of time to process what had happened, but we had just blindsided Aunt Susan. She needed time to process, and of course, she had to call her best friend. She came over, and we told her too. More questions. More tears. More hugs. My Aunt Susan always talks about making sure you have a circle of strong women surrounding you. They were part of my circle, and I now had two more women to help prop me up, hug me, and love me through this. As devastating and as uncomfortable as it was, it was the right decision to tell them. I needed them.

Later that week, Henry drove me from Aunt Susan's house to my brother's house. His best friend Jimmy, who is another piece of our patch-work quilt of a family, was standing in the driveway. He was on his way out but texted Jason from the truck asking if I was okay. I wasn't acting like myself and didn't look well. I tip-toed around the subject, as saying the words "I was raped" still didn't come easily. Jimmy texted one more time to ask if I was okay. He was worried about me. It's funny how these big, burly, tattooed men can be so in tune when something is off with their loved ones.

Jason asked again, "Are you sure you're okay?" That's when the tears started. I told him what happened. We cried together, and he gave me the longest hug in the history of brothers and sisters. To this day, I don't know if we were crying because I had been hurt, because I had just broken the big guy's heart, or both. We had a beer and hugged some more. Henry stood silently and watched this all unfold from the sidelines. The guys hugged. I texted Jimmy what happened and asked him if he could keep an eye on my brother. Of course, he would, he always did. That's what family does for each other.

The weekend rolled around and Kim, my former college roomie, came to visit. The best thing about great college roommates is they've seen you at your best and at your worst. In my case, Kim saw the aftermath of my 21st birthday celebration, and she stood by me at the altar when I married Henry. When she came to visit, there was no expectation that I would wear anything besides yoga pants and sweatshirts. Showering was still considered optional, and we didn't have to leave my house if I didn't want to. She was simply there, a quiet companion by my side, sitting on my couch. Talking when I wanted to talk and staring at the TV when I

PART 1: SURVIVING

didn't. She paid attention to my kids when I didn't have the energy to listen to their ramblings, and she ran out for ice cream when I was hungry. She provided Henry with adult conversations that I couldn't muster, and she laid next to me in my bed when I cried because I didn't want her to leave me. Neither of us are big on expressing our feelings, so that was a big one for both of us. She handled it like a champ. (Cue Dionne Warwick's "That's What Friends Are For.")

Eventually, Henry had to return to work. I was afraid to stay at home by myself. I always had to have a companion. Either he'd drop me off at my Aunt Susan's where I would take long, leisurely naps in her big comfy bed or I'd have a "Best Friend Tuesday" where Kelly would come retrieve me from Aunt Susan's and take me to lunch or out shopping. On days when he got home from work at a reasonable hour, I would get a ride over to Jason's and spend time with him and his wife. Henry also took off work to take me to counseling. Sometimes Aunt Susan would drive the hour to my house and take me. It took months before I was ready to venture anywhere alone. Try explaining THAT to your kids. It was rough.

It's funny how being in shock works. It protects you from everything. I slept like a baby the first week I was home. I managed to get through follow-up appointments with my primary care physician and my gynecologist. They both cried with me in their offices. The STD situation had been handled in the ER, but there was still HIV, HPV, herpes, and warts to worry about. Only time would tell, but the percentages of contracting any of them were small. Based on what? I'm not exactly sure, but my gynecologist was very reassuring.

Once the shock started to wear off, all these awful feelings started to emerge. Falling asleep became more difficult. Anxiety would take over my body whenever I was in a horizontal position, and my feet would feel like ice cubes, so much so they would hurt. Like clockwork, I would wake up every morning between 4AM - 4:30AM — the same time I had gotten back to my hotel room in Russia and texted Henry that I had been drugged. Sometimes I was able to fall back asleep, other times I would lie there until Henry woke up to get the kids off to school.

My days were filled with nothingness. I had no desire to do anything. Napping was my new favorite pastime. I couldn't imagine what the future looked like anymore. It was fall — my favorite time of year — and while the leaves were changing, my feelings of guilt and shame were not. I rarely showered. I lived in my pajamas. I spent a lot of time simply zoning out, which I later learned was called dissociating. My spirit was gone.

Somehow, I survived the holidays. By Thanksgiving, I was ready to talk about my experience with a few more extended family members. My not working had a lot of people wondering what was going on. I was 100% dedicated to my career, so my sudden sabbatical raised eyebrows. I opted to tell the people who were genuinely concerned with my well-being a condensed version of what had happened. The people who were just being nosey, however, got the cliff-notes explanation: "I've been traveling a lot and wanted to spend some time with the kids over the holidays." I went back to work in January. That's when the real fun began.

Part 2: Learning

THE REALITIES OF RAPE AND PTSD

*Do not confuse my bad days as a sign of weakness.
Those are actually the days I am fighting
my hardest.*

~ Unknown

Author's Note: If you're just joining us, welcome!

The Diagnosis – PTSD

By the time January rolled around, I had been diagnosed with PTSD. In addition to having experienced a traumatic event, I had all the classic symptoms, such as feeling on edge, having difficulty sleeping, and withdrawing from my daily routine. While this is pretty normal after an event like I had experienced, most people start to feel better after a few weeks or months. I, on the other hand, started to feel worse.

Kim Rhodes, my therapist, explained that symptoms lasting this long were signs of PTSD (posttraumatic stress disorder). PTSD is a mental health problem some people develop after experiencing or witnessing a life-threatening event, like war, a natural disaster, a car accident or, as in my case, sexual assault. She explained it was my body's normal reaction to an abnormal situation and it wasn't something I was simply going to get over.

I talked to my primary care physician who agreed with the diagnosis and prescribed an antidepressant and sleeping pills.

For those not familiar, there are four key criteria to a PTSD diagnosis:

1. Reliving or re-experiencing the event through bad memories or nightmares. Some people even feel like they're going through the event again (i.e. flashbacks.)
2. Avoiding situations that remind you of the event. Some people avoid talking or thinking about the event.
3. The way you feel about yourself or others changes. Feelings of shame, fear, and guilt are all quite normal. Some people avoid activities they used to enjoy.
4. Always being on guard. This can cause symptoms such as being easily startled or being on the lookout for danger. Some people have trouble concentrating or sleeping. It also causes some people to be irritable or have angry outbursts. This is called hyperarousal.

While awareness of PTSD has increased with the number of veterans being diagnosed, I didn't understand the impact it would have on my life. I also didn't realize my brain had been rewired. These reactions? Not my fault. It had nothing to do with being strong enough, brave enough, resilient enough. There are actual areas of the brain that change including the amygdala, the hippocampus, and the ventromedial prefrontal cortex. I am not going to get in depth with this, as I really don't know anything about brain function and found the research on it dreadfully boring. You can Google it if you're interested.

I also want to add the caveat that if you're reading this because you've survived some sort of trauma, please talk to a professional. PTSD is a very real, very debilitating condition and NOBODY should ever have to battle it alone.

Back to the story. I had my diagnosis. I had a few meds. I was anxious to get back to the "old me" so I talked to HR, got a note from my doctor, and headed back into the office. I was certain that getting back into the swing of things would

PART 2: LEARNING

be good for what ailed me. It would give me a reason to wake up in the morning. It would give me a purpose. It would make me feel normal again. Wrong. Wrong. And so wrong.

Living in Geneva and commuting to Chicago is about a two hour, one-way affair. After the rape, I decided I wouldn't be able to handle the crowds of strangers that come with public transportation, so I drove. I still wasn't sleeping well at night, and the drive became dangerous and daunting.

About an hour into the commute, I started pulling over into Pete's Fresh Market parking lot to take a 30-40 minute nap in my car before getting onto the expressway. I had fallen asleep on my way to work once, and it scared the bejeezus out of me. My car naps became the only way I could make it into work the 2-3 days I was going to the office each week. The rest of the days I would work from home, or sometimes, just not work at all.

Work was so much more of a challenge than I anticipated. I was constantly exhausted — physically and mentally. I was certain at times that the anxiety would eat me alive. I was going to the job that got me raped. Instead of running from it, I was driving towards it. I was with a co-worker in Russia, yet she couldn't protect me.

By the time I pulled into the parking garage each day, I was a mess. My body ached, my heart raced, and my hands shook. In the city, elevators are a normal part of everyday life. They're in the parking garage, at my office, in restaurants. For me, elevators are a trigger for panic attacks. Based on a self-defense class I took, I came to the conclusion I was grabbed from behind, most likely when getting off the elevator in the hotel. It would explain the scratched eye, the injury to my chin and the bruising on my right arm.

Picture it: a man wraps his right arm around me to grab me and uses his left hand to cover my mouth. If I struggled (which, based on the "defensive bruising" I did try to fight back), he would have pulled my head back (the bottom part of his hand on my chin), and his thumb could have easily scratched my eye. A man was in the elevator with Lynn and me the night I was attacked and, according to Lynn, he got off on the second floor with me. It's been four years, and I still can't ride in an elevator without panicking.

Once I made it to the office, there was the issue of long hallways with empty offices. Who knew who was lurking in there? We were in the process of moving office buildings, and our normally secure floors had the doors propped open with men from the liquidator company moving items in and out. The majority of my co-workers had moved before I did, so there were weeks of being in a mostly abandoned building with strange men walking up and down the hall. It was a recipe for disaster. It was my version of hell.

Another strange phenomenon also started happening the first few days I was back at work. I would be in the middle of a sentence, and my mind would shut off. I would have no recollection of what I was saying and most times, I couldn't even remember what topic we were discussing. At this juncture, it became clear I had to tell my team what had happened to me. It was a tough conversation to have, but we were a team, and I couldn't get through the business day without their support in my condition. They were great about covering for me, picking up where I left off, or prompting me on what I was saying.

However, because of this, I was hesitant to speak with clients directly. I was a Senior Vice President, Client Strategy Director. At an ad agency. Which is a communications company. My lack of communication with my clients was hurting our business relationships. I had already been off work for three months with no explanation other than I was on a Leave of Absence. Then I was back and not speaking with them.

PART 2: LEARNING

One client was on the verge of firing us, and I couldn't even pull it together enough to try to fix it. The fear of conflict had taken over my mind. Who was I? I used to live for this stuff. Fixing things is what I did. Clients loved me. And now, I sucked. And just when I thought my life couldn't get any suckier? It did. Let me introduce you to the concept of the fugue state.

Fugue state is a fancy psychological term for a form of amnesia. Specifically, it's a kind of amnesia where a person tends to travel to another town or state with zero recollection of how they got there. This isn't the spacing out kind of thing that you do on your way to work in the mornings when you've had too little sleep and don't remember driving to work. This is for real, legit, amnesia.

For example, the first time it happened I had left the office after a long day of work. I called Henry to tell him I was coming home. I left the parking garage. I "came to" at O'Hare airport, freaking out because I couldn't find my itinerary. I had no luggage. I had no idea where I was supposed to be going. I was beyond panicked. What was happening to me?

The next fugue state, I ended up at a cemetery in Bartlett (a few towns over from mine.) Another time, I drove to Milwaukee instead of Chicago. The only reason people realized I was missing was because I had missed a conference call with my boss in NY. Knowing that wasn't my usual modus operandi, he called, and when I came to, I was in Wisconsin. At this juncture, there was serious cause for concern.

I couldn't find much on fugue states in the PTSD book I had purchased and didn't know what to type in when I tried to search for it on the web. Henry was beside himself. It was another symptom he couldn't understand and swore I just wasn't paying enough attention. I made an emergency appointment with Kim Rhodes, and she helped explain it to me. I don't think either of us knew what to make of it at that point.

Because all of this was impacting my job, my boss not so subtly suggested checking myself into a hospital where they could help me work through my issues. At the very least, he asked that I talk to HR about my options. They could cover the client issues I was having, but they didn't want to carry the weight of me disappearing on my way to work or the toll it was taking on my mental state. HR recommended I find a good psychiatrist and take a Short-Term Disability Leave. I agreed. I was exhausted, I was constantly afraid, and now I was sure I was losing my mind. PTSD blows.

It's not only the big things that make living with PTSD difficult. It's the little things that nobody will ever understand. I woke up the morning of the one month anniversary of my rape with a bruise near my left eye. I'm sure there was a perfectly good explanation of how it got there, but it sent me into a complete and utter tailspin. I searched my body from head to toe making sure there wasn't any other unexplainable bruising. I swore I could still see the bruises on my knees. I knew they weren't visible to anyone else, but at the moment, they were there. I could see them. I was having a full-on panic attack. Racing heart, chest pains, sweats, shaking hands, tunnel vision, and the inability to do anything but sit on the floor and try not to die.

My startle response became unbearable. To this day, the slightest unexpected noise can send me into a complete state of panic. Thunder, the air conditioning turning on, a branch hitting the side of the house. It's gotten so bad, and my responses so over the top dramatic, that my now 13-year-old son has learned to stomp in the hallway before he gets to my room so as not to surprise me. It's annoying but a reality that we live with in this household.

PART 2: LEARNING

Exhaustion. Having PTSD can suck the life right out of my day simply because I'm always tired. I think this symptom hurts the most because it affects my family life. My kids don't want a mom that sleeps all the time. They don't understand what's happening to me, but they're old enough to see a hot button and know when to push it. The guilt they can induce is overwhelming.

The upside to this, I suppose, is that as a working mom, I always envisioned what it would be like to stay home. The reality is, I wasn't missing much. That time between them getting home from school until bedtime, really are the witching hours. They're tired after a long day, they have homework to do, they want/need to have dinner and then watch TV before it's time for them to go to bed and do it all over again the next day.

All those years thinking I was missing out on those magical mom moments were a waste of time. Being a stay at home mom is hard. Being a stay at home mom with PTSD is impossible. Thank goodness for a supportive husband who switched jobs so he could work from home.

I was still dissociating a lot at home. Again, Henry's take on it was that I was just spacing out and/or not paying attention. As I would eventually learn in therapy, neither of these assumptions are true. When I dissociate (and four years later, I still do!), it has nothing to do with anything I can control. It has everything to do with wanting to separate my mind from my triggers, or reminders, associated with the rape. For me, this is quite a laundry list:

- TV shows/movies where a character is drugged (this happens in pretty much any drama these days)!
- TV shows/movies where a woman is raped, or there's any type of violence against women

- Male British accents
- Russian accents
- Long hallways
- Elevators
- Vulnerable situations – walking in the dark, parking lots, crowds of people surrounding me
- Situations that are out of my control
- Being far away from Henry
- Shampoo in my eyes
- Unexplained bruises
- Smell of cigarettes
- Groups of people being loud/rowdy
- Sitting in public where I don't have immediate access to an exit
- Writing PowerPoint presentations
- Sitting in heavy traffic
- Hotels
- Airplanes/Airports

Being in public became very difficult. The minute something was out of my control and not going as planned, I would go off the rails. It always ended up resulting in huge, embarrassing public meltdowns.

One time the Guest Services employee at one of my favorite stores wouldn't allow me to return a $20 sweatshirt on the same day I purchased it without my receipt. She explained the system needed to reset over night before she could process the return but told me that I'd be able to bring it back the next day. I was so overwhelmed that all I could do was break out into sobs. I'm sure it freaked her out a bit, but in all fairness, she was somewhat of a bitch, and people with PTSD can have a really hard time handling conflict.

A similar event occurred when the pharmacy was having issues with my insurance and couldn't refill a prescription that I desperately needed. It resulted in me screaming like a mad woman at the pharmacist in a crying, hysterical fit of rage. Again, in all fairness, the drug they delayed filling was an anti-psychotic so being off my meds didn't help the situation.

Another time, I made reservations for my daughter and myself to have dinner at a restaurant in town. There had been a glitch in their system, and they didn't have a table for us. I had the email confirmation for our reservation! They HAD to give me a table. They did not have a table to give me, so what did I do? I put my hand on my hip, I stomped my foot (yes, literally), I yelled at the hostess, and I cried — big, ugly tears — while people were trying to enjoy their lobster ravioli and expensive glasses of wine in one of the nicest restaurants in town. Who was I and where was the always calm, always confident woman I used to be? This new version of me was acting bat-shit crazy.

Because of the "craziness," it simply became easier to disengage from life. I would spend my nights awake and my days sleeping. I avoided public places, and my lackluster approach to life alienated me from most of my "friends."

Showering, and sometimes (cough) brushing my teeth became optional. TV often triggered too many memories, so my love of Primetime television started to diminish. Watching or reading the news induced even more panic. I had no desire to travel anywhere and really didn't have much to talk about with the people who still loved me. I saw no future for myself. I was lost, and I was lonely. I didn't want to be alone, but I didn't want to have to talk to anyone either.

The question I hate the most, even to this day, is "how are you doing?" If a loved one is asking, it's because they genuinely want to know but on the flip side, do I really want to tell them that I haven't showered in four days and my new favorite hobby is laying in bed, listening to the quiet? It's a far cry from the outgoing, overly ambitious, conquer the world Brenda they knew and loved.

I stopped talking as much and moved to texting as my primary source of communication. It was easier to sound chipper that way. I could dodge the "how are you doing?" questions and still manage to keep people up to speed enough on what was going on in our world. I could give a kid update without having to talk too much about myself. Weird — my favorite subject used to be me.

By February of 2014, I began to understand why some people with PTSD kill themselves. I grew up an orphan, so there's no way I would do that to my kids, but the thought did cross my mind. If there was a way to get rid of the excruciating pain and sadness that was eating me alive from the inside, I would take it in a heartbeat.

I remember leaving Kim Rhodes' office one day and could feel the darkness spreading through my veins, I started scratching at my right arm, digging my nails into my skin trying desperately to find a way to get it out of my body. Blood came out, but the utter despair that had taken over my body had made itself at home. Believe me when I say, PTSD hurts.

It was time to start seeing a psychiatrist. I did some research and talked to my primary care physician who wasn't comfortable treating me for my PTSD after the fugue states were introduced into my life. I was desperate, so I searched and searched until I could find a psychiatrist who could see me as soon as possible. I found one, but she was horrid.

PART 2: LEARNING

She spent 30 minutes of my 45-minute appointment going through her office rules, what to do if you miss an appointment, what to do if you're going to be late for an appointment, how she handles prescription refills, and when it's appropriate (or not) to call with an emergency. She all but told me what to wear when I was coming to see her. The last 10 minutes of the appointment were spent with her ruling out my having PTSD, she didn't believe I was having fugue states and saw no reason why I couldn't go back to work. What?

I tried to explain my memory lapses, how physically draining the two-hour drive into the office was, my inability to sleep, and that I wasn't going to be able to hop on an airplane and fly to NYC every time my boss needed me to work on a project in person. She didn't believe a word that was coming out of my mouth. Quite frankly, she was a cold-hearted bitch. I was devastated and left her office feeling even crazier than when I walked in. Was this really all in my head? Why hadn't I been able to get over it? This was all my fault. I called my primary care doctor in tears. She was appalled by this doctor's "diagnosis" and asked around for referrals from her colleagues. That was how I found Dr. Shea.

Dr. Shea is another doctor I credit with saving my life. I wasn't thrilled that he was a male, but I heard he was good at what he does. There was a six-week wait to get in to see him. I felt like I was losing valuable time getting back to work but something told me to sit tight and wait for this appointment. I am so glad I did. The six-week wait passed slowly, and I was terrified to go see him.

His office was located in a local hospital at the time, which required me to park in a parking garage and then take an elevator up to see him. It was torture. I was a mess. I didn't even know where to start before the visit, so I typed out an overview of what had happened, the symptoms I was having, my overall concerns about the fugue states, and bulleted pointed out a section that simply asked for help. When I walked into his office, I handed him my write-up and waited for him to read it. I thought I had done a very thorough job, but as much as he appreciated my detailed summary, he wanted to talk about it. Sigh. Mental health experts always have so many questions.

The thing I remember most about the visit was the anxiety I had walking into his office was dissipating. He had a kind voice. He acknowledged how horrible it must have been to survive such an ordeal. He agreed instantaneously with the PTSD symptoms. He had ideas on how we could treat the fugue states. He told me I had suffered a severe trauma but that he hoped I would work with him and together we could find a solution to make living worthwhile again. I liked him. I trusted him, and I believed he could help me. It was the first time I'd felt hopeful in a long time.

It's been about three years since I started seeing him. We've tried a myriad of drug cocktails to manage my symptoms with a lot of trial and error. I have anti-depressants, anti-anxiety, and antipsychotic pills along with sleeping pills, which give me nightmares, so I have another pill that I take to keep those at bay.

I don't want to be on all these meds. They make me gain weight, and I'm tired more than I should be. Without them though, I'd be tired from always being anxious. It's like walking a tightrope. Too much one way or another will cause me to fall again, so I work with Dr. Shea every 4-6 weeks. We weigh the pros and cons of what's going on over the next few weeks and adjust as needed. Sometimes, when things are going well, I need fewer meds and sometimes, when the darkness takes over, I need more meds. I am thankful to have Dr. Shea and my meds. I can't imagine the pain and suffering that I'd still be in if it weren't for them.

PART 2: LEARNING

Again, if you're reading this and think you have PTSD, for the love of all things good and beautiful, get help. You don't have to live in misery.

Voodoo Witch Magic (AKA Somatic Experiencing)

So, I had Dr. Shea in my corner, and I was still seeing Kim Rhodes. While working with her was healing in a cathartic sense, my bodily symptoms were getting worse. The panic attacks, bouts of dissociation and the fugue states had everyone concerned. She recommended I try EMDR, otherwise known as Eye Movement Desensitization and Reprocessing. I was desperate to feel better, both physically and mentally. After doing my research on this treatment method, and the success that Veterans suffering from PTSD were having with it, I was willing to give it a shot. To be quite honest, I was willing to give anything a shot if there was any hope that I'd feel better.

I took her recommendation and made an appointment with Suzanne, now lovingly referred to as my voodoo witch doctor. It was the best decision I ever made. I should also caveat that she is not actually a voodoo witch nor is she a doctor, but she is very good at what she does.

Walking into Suzanne's office, I had a basic knowledge of what EMDR entailed (thank you Google!) but, given the magnitude of my PTSD symptoms, she recommended

PART 2: LEARNING

Somatic Experiencing Therapy as my primary form of treatment. What? Kim never mentioned this as an option, so I was slightly skeptical but completely desperate.

In short, Suzanne explained that a dude named Peter Levine came up with this theory that PTSD could be healed if we had the ability to mirror how wild animals adapt and recover from life-threatening situations. Think about it, a baby gazelle gets chased down by a lion, escapes, and goes about its day. The gazelle almost died but has the innate ability to shake it off and move on. So, if humans could tap into the same part of the brain that mammals use to discharge the excess energy once they're safe, we could re-regulate our bodies after a traumatic event.

If you've read any books on trauma, I'm sure you've read about the survival responses of fight, flight, or freeze. Somatic Experiencing takes whatever part of those responses that are still stuck in your body and helps you release them. Once that can be accomplished, your brain goes back to normal (or as normal as it was pre-trauma) and you start to feel better. If you're interested in learning more about this subject, check out Waking the Tiger: Healing Trauma by Peter Levine.

Now back to me. One of my all-time favorite sessions with Suzanne was on a day when I woke up feeling optimistic. I showered and even blow dried my hair. I'd been on a two-week run of feeling good, so when she asked how I was doing, my response was "I'm feeling happy." In typical Suzanne fashion, she asked: "How do you know you're happy?" I responded with, "I'm smiling." We went down her typical path of "Where do you feel it in your body?" and "If your body could follow that feeling what would it do?" After a bit of back and forth and a few somatic experiencing exercises, my hands began to shake. Again, in true Suzanne fashion, she told me to let them shake. Stay curious. So, I did. And the coolest thing happened. I started to feel a tingling in my fingers. I stayed curious and the next thing I knew, I could feel energy being released through my fingertips. My hands took the shape of holding a ball, and I could feel the energy running from pointer finger to pointer finger, ring finger to ring finger, pinky to pinky. It was powerful. I was excited. I felt like an X-Man. She asked what I wanted to do with the power. At first, I said I want to shatter it on the ground, so I made a throwing motion, and my imaginary ball crashed into pieces. I put my fingers back in the ball formation, and the energy was still flowing. I said, "I want to throw this power at my rapist's head!" So, I threw my imaginary ball of light and knocked him clear across the room. At that point, the energy had dissipated. I was sad when the energy release ended, but wow. I had never felt more powerful in my life. Nobody ever said her methods were conventional, but I walked out of her office like a boss. On that day, I was a certified badass.

PTSD: My New "Normal"

Anybody suffering from PTSD has quirks. Everybody suffering from it will have different quirks. Here's a list of my quirks. I don't apologize for them, and you shouldn't either. It's my new normal. I don't like them, but they're part of my PTSD baggage. It's just how I am for now.

- I have to have a water bottle with me at all times. No exceptions.
- The minute I lie down, my feet turn into popsicles. The voodoo witch doctor says they're in "freeze" mode. We've tried lots of things to unfreeze them. I consider them work in progress.
- When I crawl into bed, I cannot lie straight back. The motion of "falling" backward is too much for me. Instead, I have to sneak in sideways. From that position, I can roll over onto my back.
- Progress note: for a long time, I couldn't even rest my head against the car's headrest or the back of my couch. Suzanne did some of her freaky voodoo witch magic, and we were able to break that habit. It's nice to be able to relax and sleep on a road trip now.

- My hands are usually folded if I'm not doing something. This is because they have a noticeable tremble. I stopped getting manicures because of it.
- I avoid going out after dark at all costs.
- I used to love rain. Now it depresses me, and I usually cry.
- I can't wear coats with hoods. It disrupts my peripheral vision, and I panic.
- Sitting in traffic causes major anxiety.
- Speaking of anxiety, when it gets too bad, I sit down. Anywhere. I've sat down in the middle of the women's section at Target, on a sidewalk at Disney, in the grass at a baseball ceremony. My legs stop working and I just plop myself down wherever I happen to be at the moment.
- We have a security system for our house. I will turn it on in broad daylight if I'm home alone.
- I sleep with a nightlight.
- I carry mace like other people carry cell phones.
- I used to do "Girl Trips" with my Aunt Susan, Kelly, or my college roommates. Now I've banned myself from traveling without Henry.
- Too much noise makes my brain feel like scrambled eggs. For example, Henry can't watch TV and a video on his phone at the same time. It pains me. I haven't seen a concert since 2013.
- I don't like eating in restaurants with bars. It automatically puts me on high alert.

Tips For Managing a Panic Attack

This seems like an appropriate moment to pause and talk about the coping skills I've learned to help me survive my panic attacks. There are two that I like to use: a grounding technique and a breathing method.

The first is called a grounding technique. It starts with standing or sitting with both feet firmly on the ground. Feel your feet. Wiggle your toes. Now look around and name out loud five things you can see. Make sure you're turning your head to look for things. This will get you out of the "freeze" state that you're in. Next, look for four things you can touch — say them out loud. Listen for three things you can hear. Two things you can smell. One thing you can taste (I like to keep Jolly Ranchers on hand for this part.) Keep repeating until your heart rate and breathing slows down, the room stops spinning and whatever other symptoms you may be experiencing calm down. Keep wiggling your feet, move your wrists around, I like to move my head side to side. Give it a whirl and see if it works for you.

If that all seems like too much to manage when you're feeling like you're going to die from panic, try a simple breathing technique. Inhale for four counts, hold for four counts, exhale for four counts, hold for four counts. If four is too much for you, try three at first. The point is to manage your breathing as best as you can. If you're too dizzy to count, a simple "I'm breathing in" "I'm breathing out" can work just as well. Managing your breath can be quite effective in helping calm a panic attack. I hope it works for you, too!

THE "R" WORD

I'm going to say it. I was raped. I was raped. I was raped. I was raped. I was raped. It's still uncomfortable to say it out loud. I was raped.

Now I'm going to say It wasn't my fault. It was NOT my fault. It was not MY fault.

Why is rape such a taboo subject to talk about? If a person gets cancer, they tell people they have cancer and build a support network around them of prayer warriors and people bringing them meals. If you break your leg and require surgery, people send flowers and cheerful Get Well Soon cards. If your house gets burglarized, there's usually a community outcry to better our neighborhood, look out for each other and ask for more police patrols until the perp is caught or moves on to the next town.

But when you're raped? It's not something you talk about. It's a dirty subject. It's an uncomfortable subject. It's a subject that automatically comes with awkward silence, an "I'm sooo sorry" and always a myriad of questions — "Were you drinking?" "How much did you have to drink?" "What were you wearing?" "How'd you get yourself into such a dangerous situation?" "Were you flirting with him?" "Who were you out with?" "Are you sure you were raped? I mean, you were on a date with him." "You were drunk, are you sure it's not just a case of the 'morning afters'?" And heaven forbid the accused rapist is famous. Then you're automatically a gold-digging whore.

People ask the victim all these questions yet not one of these questions puts the accountability on the rapist. The accountability is all on survivor. Asking these questions is simply giving the victim an opportunity to change their uncomfortable story. Here's a clue — a rape survivor doesn't need the chance to change the ending and say, "you are so right, my bad, I wasn't raped." WTF?

Friends, family, rape survivors — we need to talk about this. Why does it make people so uncomfortable? No, we don't have to go into the intimate details of what exactly happened to our bodies that night, but there should be NO SHAME in talking about what happened. We were injured. We were traumatized. There is NO excuse anyone can make for raping you and then justifying it. When people ask those questions — that's what they're looking for — justification for why it happened. The sad thing is, nobody is looking for justification to build a rape survivor up. They're trying to justify the rapist's behavior to minimize how awful it is.

Do you know what I have to say about that? Fuck any person who doesn't believe you or tries to make your story more about your actions than your recovery. My personal story is that somebody slipped something into my drink and raped me (insert the condescending look and the obvious eye roll.) I was DRINKING (gasp!) on a Saturday night when I was stuck 6,000 miles away from my family. I was hanging out in the very nice hotel bar with a colleague, mingling with other people who were part of the Olympic family. And don't forget the jeans, sweatshirt, and tennis shoes I was wearing. I was asking to be kidnapped, used, and abused for some bastard's sick pleasure.

We need to change the conversation. We need to take the shame out of being raped. Over the past few months in

PART 2: LEARNING

telling people about this book, it's amazing the number of women who are raped and have never told their story. To be honest, I had a tough time at first explaining to people that I was writing a book about rape and the toll it can take on a person. It was uncomfortable for me to say out loud, but the message of this book far outweighs my comfort.

It is critical that we support these men and women, not shame them. To build them up and help them heal, not force them into hiding. There is NO excuse for raping somebody. Ever. I don't care what they were wearing, what they were drinking, how they were acting, or if they were passed out and couldn't say no. No means No means No, and if he/she/they are too out of it to say Yes, that means No too! If you have a friend who was raped or is struggling with PTSD (I'm guessing that's why you're reading this book), allow me to make some suggestions on more appropriate responses:

Believe them and say, "I believe you." Those are powerful words.

A survivor also needs to hear the sentence "This wasn't your fault."

"What you went through must have been awful. I am so sorry. When you're ready to talk about it, I'm here."

"I'm here for you, and you don't have to go through any of this alone. What do you need right now?"

Offer to go to the police, hospital, counseling with them.

Respect their decision not go to the police if that's the route they choose to go. Do encourage them to seek medical attention (asap) and counseling (when they're ready).

Don't leave them alone unless they ask to be left alone. Then stay close by in case they need you.

Keep them hydrated and try to get them to eat. Self-care is not on the top of their list. Help them care for themselves until they're ready to take on that responsibility.

When people start asking the stupid rape questions, suggest they not ask stupid rape questions. Say it nicer than I just did…or don't. We should start a movement of stupid rape questions that make normally smart people feel stupid for asking!

Be with them when they work up the courage to tell other people. My BFF Kelly helped me tell my Aunt Susan, who's like a mom to me. I didn't know if I could get the words to come out of my mouth but between the two of us, we told her. I needed my Aunt Susan to help love me through this. Kelly knew that too, and she helped me obtain it.

Help them make decisions by posing "either-or" questions. "Would you like pizza or tacos for dinner?" Making decisions can be overwhelming, especially at first. However, it's important to note that being raped is about taking away a person's power and control so having the ability to make their own choices is critical.

Don't put a timeline on healing. "It's been xxx months, shouldn't you be feeling better by now?"

Don't dismiss their anxiety, fear of certain situations or changes to their behavior or personality. Something major happened to them, it can change a person. Be respectful of this.

Guilt is a Bitch

A survivor of rape is dealing with a lot of feelings and believe me when I say, feelings suck. They hurt, and they're overwhelming. One of the toughest feelings to deal with is guilt. Guilt is that feeling that comes to us when we feel like we're responsible for what happened to us. I can say over and over again that it's not my fault, but in the back of my head, I still feel guilty. I feel guilty for:

- Drinking too much (even though I have no idea how much I drank that night)
- Being overly friendly with strangers — especially a group of guys
- Losing control, "allowing" myself to be drugged
- Doing what my rapist wanted me to do in that room that night
- Even though there were "defensive" bruises on my body, I feel guilty for not fighting hard enough
- When I woke up the next morning, I didn't believe what had happened to me was anybody's fault but my own. Yes, I feel guilty for feeling guilty

Guilt is such an intense feeling that it can make us want to numb the pain, but when we numb the pain, we numb a lot of other things too. We numb ourselves from the good feelings. The happy feelings. And the thing is — those feelings do come back. It may take a while, but there will be a moment when you realize you don't feel completely sad. Then another moment where you'll see something, and it will make you smile. And one day you'll have enough energy to go out with a friend and God forbid — you find yourself laughing.

I'm not a therapist. I can't help you shed your guilt, and quite honestly, I'm still carrying my own around, but I can tell you to acknowledge it. Put it out there. Write it down. Then imagine it was your friend who was in your shoes. Would you ever let them believe any of those things they feel guilty about was enough to justify them being raped? Think about that. It wasn't my fault I was raped, and it's not your fault or your friend's fault that you/he/she/they were raped. There is no excuse, no justification, that will ever make rape okay.

TRUST ISSUES

Another issue I've had since coming home from Russia? Trust. We're talking serious trust issues. I used to believe in the goodness of humanity. I used to believe bad things wouldn't happen to me because I'm a good person. People wanted to be around me because they liked me.

Coming home from Russia, I truly believe it was one of those men at the bar that night who raped me. I can't prove it, but in my heart of hearts, that's what I believe. So, instead of being good human beings, who just wanted to talk and laugh and have a good time, they had a very different idea of what a "good time" was going to be that night. They got close to me so they could hurt me. See where I'm coming from? I trusted the wrong guy(s).

Talk about feeling like a chump. There are basic safety rules that are hammered into your head when you go to college. Don't drink to get drunk. Never leave your drink unattended. Never take a drink from a stranger. Honestly, I don't remember how much I had to drink that night. By my count and the limited amount of time we were in the bar, I don't believe I even had enough time to get drunk. And not to brag, but this girl can handle her alcohol!

However, I did leave my drink unattended. I did take a drink from a stranger. And the thing is, I didn't think twice about it. In my mind, these guys were part of the Olympic family, and if you're part of the Olympic family, you must be a decent human being. The Olympics are about bringing the best of the best together. These guys didn't have the same ideology as I did and now I'm damaged because of it.

Since I've been home, my circle of friends has shrunk immensely. I only go out with people who I truly believe wouldn't leave me to die if somebody tried to kill me. When you use a filter like that, it definitely decreases the number of people that can be trusted. I don't go to bars without Henry, and he doesn't drink, so there's really no reason for us to go to bars, which is fine by me.

I used to love going out with my brother, Kelly, and the rest of my friends from back home, but now if we "go out" — it's out to my brother's garage to have a beer. When I go out with girlfriends, I prefer breakfast over boozing. Besides, I like to be home before dark. In my mind, the boogeyman is real. I prefer to be safely locked in my home with my big, strong husband by the time he comes out.

It's also fair to say I didn't trust my gut. I dismissed my anxiety over going to Russia. I had a really bad feeling about going on this trip. Having been to Sochi once, I knew that going without a local client was going to make this trip immensely more difficult. Henry was his usual encouraging self. Go. You'll have fun. How many people get to tour the Olympic Park before it's even been completed? etc. etc. And, the reality was, there was nobody else at the office qualified to go on this trip. I was the Olympic expert. I was the one the client wanted there to represent them. I was good at this. I was going to battle through my fear and just go.

But, as most victims do when things go terribly awry, I played the "what if" game. What if…I would have said no to the trip? What if…I had gone to my room that night instead of the bar? What if…I hadn't talked to strangers but just enjoyed a drink with Lynn instead of making every person in the bar my friend that night?

PART 2: LEARNING

What if?
What if?
What if?
What if this guy had been given a moral compass and chose not to rape me? That's the only real what if that matters. This was not my fault. Rape is NEVER the survivor's fault, no matter what the circumstances. I do trust that.

Anger

Out of all the emotions that come with being raped, anger is the one that is the hardest for me. You see, I'm a nice person. I am an optimist. I worked in advertising, an industry where the best in the business have the best poker faces. I worked for years to master mine. If we showed emotion, it was feigned enthusiasm, usually around a client's "big idea." We would smile, nod, and say we'd do our due diligence and get back to them. Then we'd look for ways to make our idea an off shoot of their idea, but better. Even on those days when our best ideas were shot down, nobody ever got angry. Drunk? Probably. Angry? Rarely.

Now here we are, more than three and a half years post-rape and bam! I'm pissed. I can feel the anger coursing through my blood. The problem is, I don't know what to do with it. My therapist has tried desperately to tap into it, but it's locked away so deep inside, I can't even get to it. I can feel it, I can acknowledge it, but I can't release it. If it hurts this much inside, I can only imagine how much it would hurt if it came raging out.

My psychiatrist asked me the other day if I was having suicidal thoughts. Hmmm. How does a person as angry as I am answer that without getting committed? I smiled, said I understood why people who commit suicide do, but that I was fine. Am I suicidal? I don't think so, but I am sad and outraged, and these feelings suck.

PART 2: LEARNING

I want to scream and cry. I want some kind of release to find my happiness again, but the tears won't come. I want to hit something, but my anxiety is too high to go to a kickboxing class by myself at night. I went to my meditation group tonight and for the first time, felt angry at the random noises people were making. Who left their cell phone on? Why is Tom moving his feet so much? Why is Amy coughing? Get some water already! The anger kept me from my high. Now I'm even more pissed and let's be real — it has nothing to do with the cell phone or Tom or Amy, it is the negative energy pent up inside me. I'm angry that I'm angry.

I don't have a solution for it as I write this book, so for now, let's just acknowledge that it's a normal reaction to an abnormal situation and move on. Sorry, I don't have more for you on this topic, but I'll warn you — if you aren't at the angry stage yet, be prepared. It's coming, and when it comes, it's the darkest dark you'll ever feel in your life.

Work in Progress

Besides my newfound anger, one of the things I've struggled most with post-rape is letting go of who I used to be and finding a way to love the new me. Before the rape, I was a badass. I was successful in my career. I mean, come on, I was working on the fucking Olympics. There's a finite number of people in my field who have had that opportunity. I had disposable income. I had a big office with floor to ceiling windows, a couch, lots of books on leadership and a team of incredibly smart people surrounding me. I had a kick-ass social life and lived it to the fullest.

My family traveled a lot. I had a work hard/play hard philosophy. It was exhausting, but I was blessed, and it was obvious. Yes, I was orphaned at a young age, but that gave me the drive that got me to the top of my career. I didn't have parents to borrow money from, I had to make my own. It was my story to write, and that book would have been about a small-town girl turned big city ad executive. I had the working mom thing figured out (as much as any mom has it figured out) and a supportive husband at home. He was my partner and life was pretty damn good. I knew where I had been and I had a firm grasp on where I was going. Then the rape happened.

Being raped changed me. It changed my views on people and how the world works. I'm afraid all the time. I am not proud of the new version of me, so I keep my circle of friends

PART 2: LEARNING

very small. It's hard feeling vulnerable all the time, so only those nearest and dearest to me get a glimpse into what my new life is like.

It's not pretty. Money is ridiculously tight. I've gained 40 pounds that I blame on one of my meds that keep me sane(ish) and my dependency on ice cream to soothe me on a bad day or to treat myself on a good day. I sleep a lot during the day. I don't shower as often as I should. Some days I don't even get out of bed. Living with PTSD and all its quirks is exhausting.

On the flip side, I've gained a new appreciation for my husband. Prior to the rape, I loved and wanted him in my life, but l didn't "need" him. He was a great dad to our kids, he kept the house going while I was off solving the world's advertising problems and he always said he loved me. He was my biggest cheerleader and I loved him for it. I always thought of him as a really nice guy with whom I was immensely lucky to share my life. He's handsome too!

Now he's my rock. He brings me ice cream when I'm sad. He tells me I'm pretty even when I haven't showered. When I'm too tired to parent, he's all over it. When I need to cry, his shoulder is always there along with a corny joke that makes me laugh. He lets me have my dark days, but he doesn't let me unpack and live there. He's taught me what it's like to have somebody to not just lean on but to trust. He's seen the darkest parts of me and loves me anyway.

Loving somebody with PTSD must be harder than living with it, I'm not sure, but he's shown me what unconditional love really is. On a lot of days, he carries the burden for both of us, and there will never be words to describe how incredibly blessed I am to have him by my side.

Since I'm currently unable to work due to my fugue states and all, I've also had the chance to spend more times with my kids. Now I'm not saying that being a stay at home mom makes me a better parent than I used to be. I truly believe I was a great working mom because it was hard to take the limited time I had with my kids for granted. I truly believe there's a difference between quality vs. quantity and quality will always win in my book.

I think that's the reason we used to travel so much. I loved the uninterruptedness of vacations vs. the routine of daily life. I loved traveling and really getting to enjoy time with my family. Thanks to daycare, my kids are incredibly social, independent and they are great problem solvers. They rarely need my help with anything, which works out well considering there are lots of days when I don't have the energy to help them.

However, I'm around more. I get to hear them interact with each other and their friends. I know their mannerisms and have become a reliable taxi service for my daughter and her gang of giggling girls. They seem to roll in packs. I've also been able to enjoy watching my son's baseball games. He's quite the talented player but my time for fandom used to be limited to weekends. I appreciate his games because it gets me out of the house and forces social interactions.

Some of the baseball moms know what happened to me. Some don't. And both are fine. My PTSD doesn't flare up at baseball games unless we're traveling for a tournament somewhere. Then some of my actions may become peculiar — like sleeping in the car during an early morning game because I couldn't close my eyes in the hotel room the night before. The tournaments are draining, to say the least, but thanks to Henry's constant companionship while we're at the hotel, I survive. It might not be easy, but that's my new life. PTSD is not easy.

Living with PTSD makes the days really long. I'm afraid to go out much by myself, so I look for ways to keep my days busy. At first, I learned how to crochet. I made my

PART 2: LEARNING

mother-in-law a beautiful scarf for Christmas one year. Truth be told, I crocheted a dozen scarves leading up to that Christmas, but that was the only one that was gift worthy. Crafting isn't really my thing.

The following year, I trained for a half marathon, mostly on my treadmill in the basement. Training was particularly hard because some days I had to go outside and run because running on a treadmill for an hour is monotonous. Running on it for 2 or 3 hours? Painful. Being outside is scary, so I would usually run with mace in my hand and to this day, I'm shocked I didn't accidentally mace myself while pushing through a tough 8 miler.

The next big project? Decorating my house. My psychiatrist explained that it was therapeutic because there was a sense of satisfaction that came with starting a room and then finishing it. I limited most of my shopping trips to when Aunt Susan or Henry's mom, Maria, could shop with me. To be honest, though, there's nothing particularly scary about Pier 1. It's a nice store that's not usually crowded. I learned to go there alone. Same thing with Hobby Lobby. The Christian music in the background is actually quite soothing. I learned that I can shop there by myself too. I am making progress.

Over time, I found a gym for women only and figured out that I can feel safe while I'm there. I've also learned to extreme coupon so going to CVS and Target by myself is an okay experience.

Each day is dictated by how I slept the night before, the amount of energy I have when I wake up and if my PTSD is going to stay tucked away in my brain and leave me alone or rear its ugly head and make me miserable for the day.

On days when leaving the house seems too overwhelming, I have learned to appreciate the quiet. When I'm not sleeping, I love reading books and have recently taken a liking to self-help books. (I'll list my favorites in the appendix in case you're looking for some inspiration for yourself.) It may be one quote of a 300-page book that makes me feel a little bit better about myself, but I'll write it down in a journal and keep referring back to it. I have a nice collection to go to when I need a pick-me-up or to feel inspired to write.

I have also found meditation helpful when my brain feels scrambled. There's something about focusing on my breathing that reminds me that I'm alive and no matter how rotten I feel, there was a moment in time when I was afraid my life was over. I will never take being alive for granted again. Even if the day is a crappy one, there's a chance the next day might be better. And I'm alive for my kids. I thank God every night for that.

Speaking of God, I recently started reading a daily devotion. The funny thing is, it's the same devotion book that my brother has started reading. He always posts a pic of the day's text and puts it on Instagram. It has now become a mental competition to read it from my own book vs. reading it on social media, but there is comfort in knowing that we're reading the same message every day. We both have our demons, we both worry immensely about each other, but we're also both relying on the same God to help us get through another day.

Lastly, I have found a couple of life coaches that I can talk to when I need a clearer focus outside of my PTSD. For example, I participated in an intention setting call this month. We talked about the differences between a goal line and a soul line, inner conflicts, success, and the concept of what if success is just being yourself? It's deep, but when you have somebody working with you step by step, you can start to connect the dots. So, for example, one of my intentions is:

This month, I am not holing myself up in the house but will look for opportunities to feel alive:

PART 2: LEARNING

- I am going to go for a walk at least once a week
- I am going to drink coffee outside on a beautiful fall day
- I am going to work out 3x a week
- I am going to go on a date with Henry
- I am going to go to a guided group meditation

There's a lot more to it. I've created a vision board to remind me of what I want my life to look like, knowing all of it is achievable. I have decided that my story is worth telling, even if it only helps one person. To acknowledge every day that I am alive for a reason. My ultimate goal is to get over my fear, but I don't know if my brain will ever let me. So, for now, I'm simply doing my best to live alongside it, find something to smile about every day, be grateful and to try to hear what the universe is telling me. The new me is a work in progress. I'm learning to be okay with that.

The Pursuit of Happiness

I want to be happy. I REALLY want to be happy. The question, though, is what does happiness look like for someone with PTSD? For me, it depends on the day. Some days, happy is as simple as a cup of really good coffee to start my day. It's getting out of bed and putting on something that actually resembles an outfit. On a really good day, it would be showering AND blow-drying my hair. Maybe even putting on make-up. That used to be my daily routine. The "old" me wouldn't have considered not showering, getting dressed, doing my hair, and putting on make-up. The new me finds those tasks optional, based on the day. On a good day, though, it could happen. And on those days, I am happy.

My favorite days are when I have a really good reason to shower, do my hair, get dressed and put on make-up. Those are the days when I'm going to leave the house to have breakfast or lunch with a friend. Those are the days that no matter how zombie-like I felt when I woke up, I am going to have to put on the face of a "normal" person. And do you know what? That's usually a really good thing. "Normal" people have friends and go out for coffee and talk about non-rapey things and smile and laugh. Or, we talk about our problems and realize, we all have problems.

PART 2: LEARNING

It's a nice reality check that I'm not the only one struggling with things. Our struggles might be different, but like they say, everyone is battling something we don't know about. Be Kind Always. Those words stick with me all the time, and I have a profound gratitude for the people in my life who are always kind to me. Most of them know what I'm dealing with, but even the ones who don't, the ones who read my Facebook posts and wonder…hmmm, what's up with her? They are still kind. I keep my social circle very small, but my handful of friends truly are some of the kindest people I've ever met.

On a lot of days, happiness is having the energy to get out of the house by myself. It's a big deal for me to do much of anything by myself. Today, for example, is a beautiful fall day. The leaves are just starting to change colors, and the air has a light crispness to it. The sun is shining. The sky is a little brighter than usual, and there's not a cloud in sight.

By my standards, this is a perfect day. The reality is though, I may never know what that air feels like on my skin. I'm dressed in real clothes. My hair is up in a ponytail. I'm presentable "enough" but I don't know if I have "enough" in me to go outside to enjoy this day. There's a part of me that wants to, but the other part of me knows it's safer to just stay inside. My energy level is on the low side today. The internal struggle on this one is real. The temptation to crack my window and crawl back into my big comfy bed with a warm blanket over me is so tempting. I am certain I'd feel better breathing in the cool air, going for a walk and getting some exercise (gasp!) but happiness might elude me today. It's going to be a wait and see.

Sometimes happiness is spending the day out and about with one of my kids. It could be walking around downtown Geneva, our cute little town that looks like it's straight out of a Dickens novel. Sometimes we'll visit the shops, find home décor to add to my wish list and grab some ice cream or a coffee at our favorite café. My teenage daughter can ALWAYS find a new outfit she wants in one of the adorable boutique or consignment shops, and we'll often stop at the Little Traveler to sample some goodies, find treasures we don't really need (but are too cute to pass up) and then take a brief moment to acknowledge how pretty our church is sitting in the center of town. I have all this a mere three minutes from my house, and yet, happiness easily eludes me.

I hate taking time for granted. We all have this finite amount of time that God has given to us. Coming from an industry where time is literally money, it's been a tough transition into time just being time. Someday, hopefully in the near future, I'll have a job again. My days will get busier. Time will become more valuable again. But for now, while I'm still trying to figure out what my new life looks like with this crazy condition called PTSD, I loathe myself for wasting so much free time.

For the first time in my life, I have free time. Time to do all of those things I noted above — enjoying a fall day, going for a walk, grabbing coffee with my daughter, enjoying our quaint town, visiting with a friend — and yet, I waste so much of it. I hide in the house. There are days I can't get out of bed. It's a waste, and it makes me REALLY frustrated with myself, even though I know certain aspects of this condition are out of my control. I think that's the real struggle, I'm not truly in control of my own happiness anymore. My happiness has always been based on carpe diem! Seize the day. Now my days are based on carpe (something)! Seize the bed!

In my pursuit of happiness, I had met with a life coach that specifically focused on life transitions. She was a quirky woman, a bit older than me, but the exercises she put us through were actually very cathartic. Let me share with you one of the things we did, which was to write a story about

PART 2: LEARNING

our perfect day. You'll see a lot of similarities between how I define happiness and what my perfect day looks like. At least I'm consistent. Here we go:

It's 8:00 on a Friday morning. I roll over and smile as I wake up to my Dwayne Johnson's Rock Clock singing to me. "Good Morning Sunshine. Yeah, that's what the Rock just said. Open your eyes, get your candy ass out of bed." I giggle and then stretch. I had a decent night's sleep. The nightmares stayed away. I grab my phone to see what's happening this morning. There was a text from Braeden telling me to have a great day. Makena's text reminded me that track practice is over at 4:30 today. As if on cue, Henry walks in with a cup of McDonald's coffee in hand. Medium. 4 creams. 2 sugars. This man knows the way to my heart. The aroma of the McCafe delights the senses, and the feel of the warm cup in my hands immediately energizes me. Henry kisses my forehead before he heads downstairs. He knows better than to try and engage me in any kind of dialogue until after I've been fueled by caffeine.

Checking the clock again, I realize it's time to get up and get dressed. I have a busy day ahead of me. Throwing on my favorite pair of yoga pants and my "I don't sweat, I sparkle" tank top, I head to FitMama for my usual Friday AM Spin and Strength class. The sky is a clear blue with a few puffs of white fluffy clouds. It's a chilly 67 degrees, but there's the promise of a perfect spring day ahead. I put on my favorite pair of cheap sunglasses and turn up the radio as Justin Bieber sings his "Mama don't like you, and she likes everyone." It makes me smile. There's so much truth in that statement. My kids are almost to that age, I hope they date well.

I walk into FitMama. Lisa is covering the kid care area and greets me with a pleasant "Good Morning!" I toss my keys into my purse and head downstairs to the bikes. "My" bike is still set to my settings, so I hop on and start chatting with Jenn about the weekend ahead. A few more "Mamas" walk in, and

I can start to feel myself getting lost in the music. Jenn directs us to "find that push point!" and we're off. Bon Jovi fills the room, and we go through a series of jumps and hills. I relish in the water breaks. We keep a steady pace but have time to catch our breath. Before I know it, the class is over. It's amazing how much faster the classes seem to go these days. I'm getting stronger. Gone are the days of not being able to keep up and cheating on my resistance settings. There's a sense of accomplishment as we stretch before we go upstairs to do more core work. I chit-chat with Cassi and Emily as we walk up the steps, joking about Wednesday's ridiculously hard boot camp. There's a camaraderie among us, and I take a moment to appreciate how much I've come to look forward to these workouts.

Sweaty, yet satisfied, I hop into my car to head home. I enjoy the last few sips of cold water from my water bottle and decide the weather is worthy of rolling down my window. What the hell? My hair is already messed up, and the breeze feels good against my sticky skin. I walk inside the house on my fatigued legs. Henry is at the dining room table, hard at work. His business is finally getting off the ground. He's on the phone with a customer, so I kiss his cheek and squeeze his shoulder. I get his million-dollar smile in return. "I love that smile," I think to myself as I head upstairs for a shower. I turn on the radio and can't help but grin when a Gin Blossom's song starts to play. Henry and I saw them perform at Epcot a few years back. It was such a carefree, perfect night. I sing along and decide to treat myself to the expensive shampoo I keep in my shower for special occasions. As I dry off, I take my time to appreciate the rosy glow of my skin. My new skin care regimen is working, and I have to say, I look good. A little makeup and I'm ready to head back out the door.

I walk into the local Mexican restaurant to find the baseball moms already seated. Chips and salsa are on the table and margaritas are being delivered as I am greeted with smiles and hugs. These women, who I used to spend every summer with at

PART 2: LEARNING

the ballfields, still hold a special place in my heart. Our kids no longer play together since Braeden moved to a more competitive team, but the bond of years' past still holds strong. We catch up on everything from husbands to players, siblings to summer plans. I order my favorite carne asada tacos and simply enjoy being in the presence of these women. I miss them terribly, but for today, I am one of them again. It feels like home.

When we're done indulging ourselves on Mexican cuisine, a few moms head out, but Jill wants to walk along Third Street. Who am I to say no? It feels good to stretch my tired legs as we head outside. I inhale the fresh air and am once again filled with contentment as I look at our quaint little town. We hit our usual favorite shops and decide a treat in is order. So, we stop for an Affogato at All Chocolate Kitchen. This is why I love living in Geneva.

We say our goodbyes. I still have an hour before the kids need to be picked up from school, so I head back home and sit on my recently refurbished patio set. A sense of satisfaction kicks in as I appreciate the bright red color of the paint I chose. "It was a good call," I think to myself, as I crack open a bottle of water and turn my attention to Facebook. After scrolling through my newsfeed, filled with recipes, pics of pets and funny memes, I decide to text Kelly. She should be off work by now. "Hey. Watcha doin'?" I type. I see the bubbles of a response, so I patiently wait for her reply. "Schoolwork," she says. I swear she's been in school for at least a decade now. I also know, she's easily distracted when doing school work. ☺ I send her a funny BFF pic, which leads us down memory lane of our girls' fishing trip we took a few years back. Our text messages always get a little silly and the next thing I know, I'm laughing out loud on my front porch. We both agree we need a Girls Night In soon. After several attempts and working around three boys' baseball schedules, we agree to a BFT (Best Friend Tuesday) in two weeks. It's not exactly what we need, but for now, we'll make do. I can't wait to see her. I finally relent and let her get back to her homework and head out to pick the kids up from school.

Picking up the kids from school can go one of two ways — they're either both happy or both cranky. Today I lucked out. Makena was asked to help the teacher make guacamole in her Food Sciences class, and Braeden's team won their volleyball game in PE. Apparently, the sunshine and fresh air of a Friday caught up with them too. Good moods are contagious. Since everyone is happy, I agree to an impromptu Starbucks run. The car is filled with chatter about the day and the weekend's plans. Thankfully, nobody has anything planned tonight, a rare occurrence when you have teenagers in the house!

We arrive home. Bookbags and empty Starbucks cups are carried into the house. Henry has unloaded and reloaded the dishwasher, and the counters have been wiped down. There's nothing better than a clean kitchen. The blue sky is calling so I ask Henry if he wants to go for a walk. The kids want to join in too, so we take advantage of the weather and head over to the Fox River. The trees are finally turning green, and the path is humming with other residents of Geneva. We're not the only ones who think it's too nice to stay inside. The kids walk ahead and are filling each other in on the day's events. An occasional burst of laughter can be heard, and it reminds me of my relationship with my own brother. My heart is happy to see them so close. I say a quick prayer that they stay that way. Henry grabs my hand, and we walk in silence as we hear the river running over a fallen tree. It's peaceful. I am content.

As we drive home from our walk, the sun is starting to set. Pinks and purples fill the sky and the shadows of the day start to set in. We agree that we'll order a pizza for dinner. Score one for me — no cooking. Braeden asks if we can have a family movie night. Henry and I agree and ask the kids what they want to watch. Of course, they both agree on *Just Go with It*. They always choose *Just Go with It*. Henry and I sit on the couch

PART 2: LEARNING

while Makena takes over the corner chair and Braeden grabs pillows and blankets to make a nest on the floor. The lights are dimmed, and Adam Sandler and Jennifer Aniston take over the screen. The dog lays down at my feet. I take a sip of the Sauvignon Blanc I poured for myself. Its crisp flavor dances on my tongue. I am happy with my choice. I settle in, and Henry puts his feet on my lap. This is the life.

After the movie is over, the kids know it's time for bed. They head upstairs to brush their teeth. I do the same. It's been a long day, and I'm ready to battle the darkness that comes with bedtime. Thankfully, Henry is ready for bed too. We tuck the kids in, and I get a hug from Makena and a kiss from Braeden. The hallway light is shut off. We set the security alarm, and I'm as safe as I'm going to get. I quickly take my meds, wash my face, and brush my teeth. I take a deep breath and crawl into bed. Henry is already there. He's cracked the window and the fresh night air streams through the screen. I take one last deep breath, roll onto my side, and wait for Henry to snuggle in behind me. His foot is on my foot, and his arm is wrapped around me. I take a moment to reflect on how normal the day was. Not just normal, but pleasant. It was even more than pleasant, maybe it was almost perfect. A feeling of contentment that I rarely experience washes over me. My body relaxes, I sink a little deeper into Henry's arms. I close my eyes, and I drift off to sleep. The end.

I want this kind of happiness. I want simple, easy, normal days like this. I want to have the energy to workout consistently. I want to leave the house. I want the peacefulness that this story exudes. This is my definition of happy, and I want it back — sooner rather than later, preferably.

If you're struggling with finding your own happiness, try writing out what your perfect day looks like. Pick one thing from your story and do it for yourself. I'll do the same. Deal?

Worth noting: I typed this whole section without giving up and crawling back into my bed. Score one for me.

Part 3: Living

Journal Entries of a Survivor

Just because today is a terrible day doesn't mean tomorrow won't be the best day of your life. You just gotta get there.

~ Unknown

Journal Entry: Introduction

Hey, friends! In this section, I've included stories from my journal, as well as my Facebook page called Brenda G Author. It's meant to talk about things related to this journey called life. As you know from previous sections of this book, I've put mine "on hold" for the past four years. It's time to start rediscovering what's out there. From working out to meditating to researching to walking with Jesus (yep, that happened!), this section will cover the topic of PTSD with as much honesty, humor, grace, and love as I can muster. Sometimes it's light. Sometimes it's dark. Join me. Maybe we can get a "two-for-one" from something I learn!

Journal Entry: The Darkness

PTSD is a bitch. It's reared its ugly head again, and the darkness is swallowing me whole. I can't leave my bed. I don't even care to turn on the lights. The curtains are closed, and the blinds are shut. The dreariness matches my mood. I'm tired. Exhausted is a better word. Exhausted physically. Emotionally. Spiritually. It feels like it's killing me from the inside out. I've slept 16 hours today. When I'm awake, I cry. I don't even know why I'm crying. Today I think it's a sad cry, not an angry cry. As the tears roll softly down my face, I wait for my pillow to envelop me again to take me away into a darkness where I don't have to feel. Henry brings me coffee and ice cream. He kisses my head. He tells me tomorrow will be better. It has to be hard to love me. I don't even love myself. He shields the kids from it as much as possible. Deep down, I wonder if they know I'm broken? I want to be better. For him. For them. For me. Today's just not the day it's going to happen. I can't wait til bedtime. When I say my prayers, I'll ask God for tomorrow to be a better day. For some peace from the sadness. For the energy to get out of bed. Even if it's just for a day. I need it to be better.

Journal Entry: Creativity

I used to work in advertising, and I LOVED it. My job was to work with the creative team to take their ideas and bring them to life. I put the ads in places where people would see them. Whenever there was a brilliant idea, I would get a high off it. It's what made my job fun. Now that I'm on this new journey to find where I'm going next, I'm scared. I'm writing and researching. I pulled out my glue stick last night and got creative with a vision board. I'm getting high on ideas. The fear? That this buzz won't last. That the PTSD is going to pop up and shut me down. So tonight, I'm going to meditate. I'm going to relax my body and live in the present. I'm not going to let the fear weigh on my mind. Then I'm going to say a little prayer, thank God for helping me find so much happiness today and then I'm going to go to sleep. May we all find peace tonight. Sweet dreams.

Journal Entry: The Power of Touch

I knew it was going to be a tough day from the moment I woke up. My anxiety level was off the charts. It's never a good day when you wake up anxious. At first, I thought it was because I had overbooked myself. A 9:15 Pilates class and then an 11:00 appointment with the voodoo witch doctor. I would have to leave Pilates exactly at 10:15, rush to Naperville and then delve into the tough stuff with my therapist. It seemed like too much, so I texted my Pilates instructor and explained I'd overbooked myself. The anxiety still wouldn't subside. Huh. So, I tried a Calming Anxiety Meditation off an app on my handy dandy iPhone. I usually choose a 10-minute meditation but knowing how bad I felt, I opted for 15 minutes. That should do the trick. Nope, not a chance. To add insult to injury, I developed a migraine over my left eye on top of the shaking body and racing heart. This was just not good. I didn't think driving to Naperville in this condition was a responsible decision. I texted the voodoo witch doctor and told her I had a migraine and needed to cancel. I never cancel on her, even on days when I really don't want to go. I know her special kind of therapy helps. I crawled back into bed, resigning myself to the fact that today was just going to be a crap day.

PART 3: LIVING

Henry had also crawled back into bed and was only half awake when he reached over and put his hand on my arm. All of a sudden, the anxiety started to subside. My stabbing headache turned to a dull throb. The shakes started to calm, and my heartbeat was slowing back down. All of this from the simple touch. I think it's something we, as a society, don't do enough. We're so busy running the rat race that we forget to stop and enjoy the benefit of human contact.

I remember when I was little, my Gram always loved touching my hands. She'd gently reach out for one of mine and just hold it while we talked. I always loved talking with her. There was an unexplainable sense of closeness. Her hands were always so soft, just like Henry's were today. I think she was onto something.

Try it with somebody you love today. You might like it, and it might be just what you needed and never even knew.

Journal Entry: Can't

In the spirit of keeping it real, today sucks. I just "can't" today. Can't shower. Can't go out. Can't parent. Can't find the energy to cook. Can't be social. It's a perfect, sunny, fall-like day and it's Geneva's Taste of the Vine festival. This gets me down even more because I feel like I'm wasting it. I want to enjoy it, I just can't. Today is about surviving. Tomorrow I will try again.

Journal Entry: The Water Taxi

I've been feeling pretty good lately. The sunshine makes my days a little cheerier, and even on dreary days, I might still be able to find a smile. I've been living in the darkness for so long that I don't even remember if this is how I used to feel prior to Russia.

I have vague recollections of being on the Chicago River water taxi on my way to work on a beautiful morning, watching the sun reflect off the city's amazing architecture. I would always take pictures on my way to the office. My love for the water taxi was well documented on social media. The perfect blue skies, the calmness of the river, there really was no better way to start the day. Those pics pop up in my Facebook Memories, and I remember how it felt to have the warm sun shining on my face along with the breeze from the speed of the boat blowing my hair. There was something about the water taxi that just made the days brighter and my steps lighter.

I think that's how I'm feeling now — brighter? lighter? I want to cut back on some of my meds. They numb the bad feelings, but they numb the good feelings too. I so desperately want to feel alive again. I want this happiness to last but that's the thing about PTSD, it sneaks up behind you and smothers you. You can't see, you can't breathe, you have to fight for air.

It's always lurking. I'm always afraid. It attacks when you're least expecting it. So even on these happy days, I don't trust my feelings. I cautiously enjoy them but am always anticipating the bottom dropping out from under me. This is no way to live, but this is my reality. So, I'll cherish these little glimpses of happiness, hope they last and keep praying for peace. It has to be out there somewhere. Maybe someday I'll be able to feel the same joy I had riding the water taxi. The water taxi kicks ass.

Journal Entry: My Mom

Wow. So tonight, I realized it was the 21st anniversary of my Mom's death. It's not that I'd forgotten that September 7th was the day she died, I honestly didn't realize that today was the 7th. More importantly, though, I stopped making it a "sad day" a long time ago. I keep my memories of her tucked in my pocket. They're always with me. When I have problems adulting and have a "What would Patti do?" moment, I pull one out and decide if that is the best or worst route to go (with my Mom it was 50/50). Then I go about my day.

Today was just like any other day, but my Mom would have loved the conversation I had with my BFF Kelly this morning. We were laughing, crying, and celebrating our friendship. My mom LOVED Kelly. It was a fitting way to kick-off the day.

The irony in all of this is the reason I didn't pay attention to the calendar was that I was busy researching PTSD all day. There HAS to be a book that is going to give me that one tip or trick I need to get over this hurdle. 334 pages later — I came up with the same answer — time. Time WILL heal me. I may not choose to carry these memories around in my pocket, but they'll be stashed away somewhere. In the meantime, I'll just keep doing what Patti would do — I'll keep trying. It's all she ever asked of me.

Journal Entry: Questions

I read a lot this weekend. It's funny, though, how looking for answers always leads to more questions:

I'm feeling pretty good, when am I going to feel like crap again? (I actually cried over this! Henry is a patient man.)

When do the lows go away? Do they go away?

What would I feel like without all the meds?

Will I ever get off the meds?

When, if ever, will I feel like "me" again?

If the old me is gone forever, what does the new me do next?

The only answer I could come up with is that there is no crystal ball. So, I'll live in the now and pray for patience and peace. It's the best I can do.

To be continued…

Journal Entry: Walking with Jesus

There was a weekend when I ran out of Risperidone, one of the more important drugs in my arsenal to manage my PTSD. I was worried about how the weekend would go. Would my anxiety be out of control? Would I be in a constant state of panic? Would there be withdrawal symptoms? After a horrible night's sleep, I woke up feeling exhausted and panicky. I'm not sure if it was a physical or mental symptom, but does it really matter? I felt like crap.

I had just started practicing meditation, so I went to that tool in my toolbox of coping strategies. I set my app to a 15-minute meditation called Calming Anxiety, worked on my breathing, and staying present with my breath. There was a calm and sense of peace when I was done. The panic had subsided, and I was feeling rested. Energized. Maybe I would be okay after all. I popped two ibuprofens to hold off any potential headaches and decided to make the most of my day.

I decided to go for a walk. It's something I try to do daily. But this day was different. Rather than listening to an audiobook or one of my iTunes playlists, I opted for quiet. I was going to stay present in my walk. I wasn't going to focus on the fear that can so easily take over my mind and/or body, and I cleared my head of worries about my day. It was then that I began to notice things. The magnificent oak tree that stands in one of my neighbor's yards. The laughing of kids racing their bikes in the driveway. The scampering of a squirrel with a nut in his mouth, jumping fearlessly into a pine tree. The welcomed cool breeze that would blow against my skin on an otherwise humid August day. When my mind started to wander to a to-do list or something unproductive, I made the conscious decision to refocus my energy on just being present in the moment. It was as if I had never taken a walk before. It was different. It was spiritual.

As I walked, my thoughts turned to God. Recently, I started to feel as if my connection to him had been lost. As I walked, I tried to talk to him, but it was awkward. Uncomfortable. Now, the God I was raised to know and love is a kind and loving God. A Father who will always welcome his child home, even after she's taken a break from their relationship. It was weird to feel alone as if I had called him on his cellphone and he sent me to voicemail. Something was off.

Instead, I called on his Son, Jesus. I like to think of Jesus as my long haired, hippy spirit guide. He understands sinners. He loves them. He befriended them when he was on earth. He died for them. For me. So, I said a silent prayer and asked him to walk with me. I even scooted to the right side of the sidewalk so he could walk next to me. It seemed silly at first, to make physical space for Him, but that's when I felt Him with me. He was there. A comforting hand on my shoulder. We didn't talk about anything. I pointed out things I appreciated God making — flowers, various types of trees, another little squirrel collecting nuts for the winter but there was no deep or profound conversation. It was just nice to have Him by my side. I tried to think of hymns from my childhood that had to do with walking with Jesus, but I couldn't come up with any. So, I went with my old standby

PART 3: LIVING

of "I am trusting thee, Lord Jesus, trusting only thee. Trusting thee for pure salvation, great and free." I wish I had something big to talk to him about today, but I didn't. I just needed a friend to walk with, and Jesus seemed to fit the bill. 4.5 miles later and I was feeling blessed.

Journal Entry: The Presence of Fear

I was reading a book last night called *The Universe Has Your Back,* by Gabrielle Bernstein and this passage stopped me in my tracks. "The presence of fear is a sure sign you are trusting in your own strength" Wow. Think about that — how many times a day do we get caught up in this? It reminded me of one of my favorite Bible verses "Be still and know that I am God." Psalm 46:10 (NIV).

So, this morning I went for a nice long walk followed by a guided meditation where I left feeling refreshed, loved and at peace. Take a moment today to let go of your worries. Find a quiet place in your mind and let the weight of your world float off your shoulders for a bit. Trust me. Trust God. You'll feel better. I promise. Have a beautiful day.

Journal Entry: Medicated

To give you an idea of what PTSD looks like, I take nine pills every night before bed — these are supposed to help me sleep, help me function, help keep the panic at bay. Yet I'm exhausted. It's been four years, and I still can't sleep at night. I prefer to sleep during the daylight hours when Henry is downstairs. Last night was rough. This afternoon's nap was awesome. I struggle with my lack of motivation on days like this — I had a million things to do to get ready for this week but oh well. All I can do is try again tomorrow. Tonight, like every night, I'll pray for patience, peace, and a little bit of sleep. I'll do the same for all of you.

Journal Entry: Change

There are changes coming soon in our household. Change is inevitable, but it's also scary. For someone with PTSD, it shakes you to the core. I've spent a lot of time hiding from the world this week, contemplating what the future holds for us, what I can do to control it and how I will cope with what is out of my control. I don't think it's a coincidence that when I opened up my devotion book tonight, this was the verse that appeared:

"Fear not, for I am with you; be not dismayed, for I am your God. I will strengthen you, yes, I will help you, I will uphold you with My righteous hand." Isaiah 41:10 (NIV).

My body may feel otherwise, but in my heart, I know I'm going to be okay. Change happens. God is good.

Journal Entry: God is Good

At the beginning of October life was getting stressful. It was all things that were out of my control. My Long-Term Disability was going to run out, we were losing our health insurance, there were problems with my Workers Comp and the checks that keep this house running weren't showing up with no explanation. I could have held onto these worries and fears, but I handed them over to God — every day and every night. Miraculously, a random check from a random source showed up in the mail on the same day I was sure we weren't going to be able to pay our mortgage. Henry was able to find us affordable health insurance. By the grace of God, we're going to be okay. None of the solutions that came our way and their perfect timing make earthly sense. I couldn't have made any of this happen on my own, but I know that brighter days are ahead.

"Then Jesus said to his disciples: Therefore, I tell you, do not worry about your life, what you will eat; or about your body, what you will wear. Life is more than food, and the body more than clothes. Consider the ravens: They do not sow or reap, they have no storeroom or barn, yet God feeds them. And how much more valuable you are than birds! Who of you by worrying can add a single hour to his life?" Luke 12:22-25 (NIV)

Keep the faith people. God is good. Take care of each other.

Journal Entry: When?

For the love of God, it's been four years, and I'm STILL not better. How long will this last? WHEN will I feel like normal again? I have good weeks and then bam! — out of nowhere, I get hit upside the head with a baseball bat and completely knocked off my feet. For example, I was on Facebook yesterday and received a friend request from a guy named Mark. The last name is irrelevant. I didn't know him, and his profile didn't give me any information — what he does for a living, where he's from, anything that could give me a clue if this was my rapist.

I know there was a guy in the bar named Mark that night. I know what he did for a living. I have a rough idea of where he's from in the UK. I know whoever hurt me had access to my Passport while I was passed out. He knows my first and last name. He knows my date of birth. All of this information is part of my Facebook profile. If he was looking for me, he could find me.

I, on the other hand, know nothing about him. It terrifies me. To get a friend request from a stranger sent chills down my spine and froze me in my tracks. I couldn't sleep. I prayed for peace over and over and over again.

According to my Fitbit, I slept for less than four hours, restless for more than five. I'm pretty sure it was the longest

PART 3: LIVING

panic attack in the history of panic attacks. I popped an emergency Xanax this morning, changed my plans for the day and tried to sleep. Still nothing. I am physically, emotionally, and mentally exhausted.

Henry looked up the troll who had sent me the friend request and decided he was just that, a guy trolling for women (and I'm astounded by the fact that women accept these requests, but I'm not here to judge). I don't want to live my life in fear, it's just a reality that comes with PTSD. I will continue to pray for patience. And for peace. And for a restful night of sleep. If you could send one up for me tonight too, that would be awesome. I am so tired.

Journal Entry: 25 Days of Zen

Henry has gone back to an office job and is no longer working out of the house. This has had a huge impact on me physically — including increased heart rate, and my normally low blood pressure is extremely high.

Mentally I'm trying to stay strong and keep busy, but when your body succumbs to physical symptoms, it's a challenge. Now I'm constantly obsessing about how awful my body feels. I decided I can't live like this for 24 hours/day, 7 days/week. So, for the month of December, from now until Christmas, I am going to make it a priority to incorporate various relaxation techniques into my day, every day.

My first experience this month was attending a free guided meditation on Thursday night. It actually increased my anxiety because it was after dark, in a new environment with a lot of new people — none of which is good for PTSD. However, now that I'm more familiar with the surroundings, I'll try again next week. The meditation itself was lovely. Once my body settled into my breath, I was able to relax. I repeated "I am safe. I am loved. I am calm." As I started to relax, I could feel a warmth wrap around me. It could have been God, my parents, an angel, or just the feel-good energy in the room, but it was very comforting. I will definitely be going back.

PART 3: LIVING

Friday's adventure was to the same location I was at for the meditation on Thursday night, but this time it was to experience Halotherapy, which is sitting in a room full of dry salt that is turned into an aerosol form so you can breathe it in. I was skeptical at first, afraid I'd get bored just sitting there for 45 minutes, but the room was very relaxing, and I lucked out with a free 15-minute guided meditation thanks to another client who was also using the room.

The chairs reclined, the light was soothing, and there were even warm, fuzzy blankets in case I got chilly. When the light turned on indicating my time in the room was over, I informed the front desk that I'd like to move in. They don't have pricing for that, so I signed up for a four-session package. The price per session ended up being less than $15 each, so that's within my budget. Score. Can't wait to go again.

The first Saturday of every month is my favorite because a woman the Universe introduced me to, Debbie, leads a healing heart guided meditation followed by yin (stretchy) yoga. It's in an awesome yoga studio, with comfy bolsters and blankets and blocks — anything you need to be comfortable for both classes. There were two new people, myself and Debbie. It was a beautiful meditation.

Debbie used the analogy of being on the monkey bars. If the first rung on the monkey bar is fear, we have to let go with one hand to move forward and then let go with the next hand to keep moving forward on our journey. It's scary to let go of that first rung, but the joy you find in your strength as you let go of that fear and keep moving forward is worth it, right? It really put me in a rejuvenated mindset. I love the small class size, and how refreshed I feel when I leave there. I treated myself to a vanilla latte from the cute little coffee shop down the street from the yoga studio and went about my day.

Sunday's event was supposed to be Quartz Crystal Singing Bowls, but the event was canceled due to the snow. I tried to meditate at home but without fail, I'd start, and somebody would walk into the room. My blood pressure was high, and I wasn't feeling well. The snow was pretty so we'll focus on that as our positive. We also drove through the Mooseheart campus as a family to look at Christmas lights. The snow only made it prettier. It's such a fun tradition, and I'm glad we got it in this year.

Day 5: Today I went for a 90-minute massage. Enough said.

Day 6: It wasn't how I planned to spend my day, but I went with the flow, and good things happened. Tonight, I listened to a few chapters of Miracles Now by Gabrielle Bernstein while enjoying a cup of (decaf) tea followed up with some quiet prayers in a quiet house. It was a good day.

Day 7: I went back to the free meditation I found. It was a rough day from a PTSD perspective, and I didn't get out of bed for most of the day. I didn't want to go out tonight but promised myself I'd do something relaxing every day, so I honored that commitment to myself and went. I am so glad I did. I released a lot of emotions I was holding onto — that's something I don't do very often. It was weird to be teary in a room full of strangers but if they were doing it right — their eyes were closed too. It can be our secret.

Day 8: Breakfast and shopping with my Mother (in law). For some people that would cause stress. For me, it made my heart happy. I am blessed.

Day 9: Error...

PART 3: LIVING

Day 10: I published my GoFundMe page for my book and let out a really big breath. It was huge.

Day 11: Spent the AM at my new favorite spa talking about my book, learning some new meditation techniques, and making a new friend. I am so thankful to have found a new "home" to relax, rejuvenate and connect with kindred spirits. I am so grateful for the people and places God has introduced me to in the past year. I am feeling so blessed today.

Day 12: Talked to an old friend and took a really long nap. It was awesome. Sleep is always better during the daylight.

Day 13: Therapy with the girl who colors my hair. Always fun catching up. She's been my go-to for at least 10 years…so lucky to call her my friend.

Day 14: My weekly group meditation. My mind was going a little nuts with all of the book excitement, holiday to-dos, and kid stuff, so it was hard to calm my mind, but when I did, it was amazing. Love meditating.

Day 15: Spent the day with Aunt Susan and her cousin, Jill, wrapping presents and chatting away. Lots of love was shared today.

Day 16: Just a day of rest. It's all I could muster.

Day 17: I am now the proud owner of a 15-lb. therapeutic weighted blanket. "These blankets work by providing input to the deep pressure touch receptors throughout the body. Deep pressure touch helps the body relax. Like a firm hug, weighted blankets help us feel secure, grounded, and safe." I am so blessed that my friends, Melissa and Margaret, spent the entire day at my house making this blanket for me. It was an 11-hour project. A lot of love went into this blanket. I am SO EXCITED. This will help so much on days when my PTSD or anxiety is out of control. And…it's CUTE!!

Day 18: I tried out yoga with crystal bowl sound healing in a salt cave. Not something you do every day. We used essential oils, did some reflexology and then some relaxing, stretchy yoga moves. The crystal bowl performance was trippy. Having PTSD, I'm very sensitive to sound, so it took a while to relax, but when I did, it was awesome. Definitely something I'll try again.

Day 19: I met with the volunteer coordinator at Mutual Ground, the rape crisis center where I plan to volunteer. There's an interview process (I passed!) but the reality of what they do really sunk in. It was not a Zen day but an important one nonetheless. I am thankful for the opportunity to give back.

Day 20 and 21: My anxiety is running at an all-time high. It's hard to function, and it's hard to adult. Self-care is key on days like these. Lots of naps, snuggling with my weighted blanket and some time meditating at the Salt Spa has helped immensely. I also called my doctor today — sometimes you just need to ask for help. We're switching up some meds, which I didn't want to do, but I'm sucking it up so I can be more present for my family. I am going to bed tonight feeling blessed for the amazing support system I have in my life. Tomorrow I've got to get with the program. Christmas is coming whether I'm ready or not.

PART 3: LIVING

Day 22: It was a CRAZY day filled with shopping and wrapping and more shopping. I did get a much-needed nap in, and now I'm resting in bed, enjoying the new beeswax candle I bought myself for Christmas. It's infused with Lavender Essential Oils, and it's amazing. Did you know Bees Wax candles not only smell great but they actually clean and purify the air when burning? Win-win-win.

Day 23: I had a date night with Henry. I love that guy.

Day 24: I spent the day with my family and capped it off with a beautiful Christmas Eve service including Silent Night via candlelight. Always makes me teary.

Day 25: We spent the day with Henry's family celebrating Jesus' birthday. Now enjoying a quiet night in front of the fire. Looking forward to bed and enjoying the soft glow of my new salt lamp.

Well, folks, it was a fun experiment. I think it's safe to say that we should all try to be kind to ourselves every day. I know that life gets hectic, but even taking the time to meditate for 10 minutes every night or spending some time talking to God can be therapeutic. Did it cure my PTSD? No. Did it give me something to focus on besides my PTSD? You betcha. Will I do it again? Most definitely.

Journal Entry: Reassurance About Writing this Book

"You're not a victim for sharing your story. You are a survivor setting the world on fire with your truth. And you never know who needs your light, your warmth, and raging courage." - Alex Elle

Journal Entry: More Voodoo Magic

PTSD — I've had a string of really good days then yesterday hit me like a Mack truck. I walked into the voodoo witch doctor's office feeling tired, annoyed, and annoyed with being tired. It was a good session — so much so that I was able to see the colors in the sunset this evening. Tonight, I'm not seeing gray. What a gift.

Journal Entry: Reiki? Yes, Please!

In the midst of my "woe is me" day, I almost forgot I had a Reiki session scheduled at the Salt Spa. I was a little apprehensive about going. Given my depressed state of mind, I contemplated canceling. It was an expensive experiment, and I didn't want to "fail" because I wasn't in the right mindset. I went. Holy hell it was freakin awesome!!! Based on my physical responses, the reiki got my energy flowing, my chakras are realigned, and I am at peace. Maybe today won't be a wash after all. I'm digging all this connecting with the Universe stuff.

Journal Entry: Wish

I wish people could understand the debilitating nature of PTSD. I have three REALLY fun projects to work on today. Super excited about all of them…but today I just can't. My body is saying "nope, not happening." So, I am crawling back into bed, under my weighted blanket, and trying not to feel sorry for myself or angry that I "just can't…" I'll try again tomorrow.

Journal Entry: More Voodoo Witch Magic

It started out a rough day. We were having our home security system updated which meant having service contractors in our home, i.e. strange men wandering around my house. Thankfully, Henry was home, but my anxiety was through the roof nonetheless. I had an appointment with the voodoo witch doctor. It took even more energy than usual to get up and out of the house to go see her. Wow, am I glad I did.

As we worked through our usual process, she started performing EMDR with a finger puppet of Bumble, the abominable snow monster from the Rudolf movie (I never said she was conventional.) A huge discharge of energy came up through the form of rapid blinking. While blinking annoys me, my left eye suffered pretty extensive trauma, so I'm never surprised when the blinking starts. While my eyes were doing their thing, my hands started to ball up, not in a punching form but a grabbing form — like grabbing somebody by the shirt collar or around the neck. Suzanne handed me a pillow and provided some resistance. I choked the shit out of that pillow. Then when she let go, I beat the pillow in my lap. The energy rush was amazing.

Instead of being afraid of all the feelings pent up inside me, I started to embrace them. After releasing my anger on the pillow, I thought I'd had my big "ah-ha" moment for the day and would get going. Nope. While talking with Suzanne, enjoying the afterglow of beating a defenseless pillow, my hands moved into a prayer mudra position. As the left hand approached the right, I could feel the energy coming off my hands. They were HOT. My feet were warm. My feet are ALWAYS cold. Whatever was happening was pretty cool. So, I went with it. I stayed curious, and I had what I'll call an inner body experience. I could feel the energy following my blood flow — down my arms, up my arms, down my legs, into my feet, up my legs.

She asked if I could put a color to it. It was a glossy bright cherry red. As I felt the energy pulsing through my veins, my hands disappeared. They were translucent. I could feel this amazing energy coming from them, but it was like they were ghost hands. WTF was happening??? It was the opposite of meditating, which is more about finding the quiet from the inside out. This was feeling the "noise" from the inside out. It's hard to explain if you're not familiar with somatic experiencing but if you've heard the terms fight, flight or freeze, my body has been stuck in freeze mode for 3+ years. I've had a couple of big breakthroughs with Suzanne but have always held my emotions back. They're stuck in my body, but I've been too afraid to tap into them. Fear is a scary emotion. Pain is a terrifying emotion. Lack of control? I can't even talk about it. Today I didn't have to — my body did it for me. Success. It feels fucking good.

Journal Entry: Meditation

What a good day for self-care. Wonderful guided meditation at the salt spa. I get why meditation is called a "practice" as I seem to be getting better at it each week. It's pretty neat to be able to shut out the noise. Now I'm laying in bed with my weighted blanket, with the glow of my salt lamp and a lavender infused beeswax candle. Just breathe…

Journal Entry: Optimism

So, I started this YouTube three-day masterclass on different meditation techniques. Pretty cool since I'm still new to this practice! Tonight's was about letting go of the complexities we form in our mind and our bodies that don't need to be there. Let's be real, I could have spent hours on this. Thankfully it was only 10 minutes but it was so enlightening. I let go of some of the darkness and accepted more of God's warmth and love. I've spent the past three years letting fear and darkness control my body and mind. This year, I intend to fight back with the light God gives us. I'm taking my body back. I will not be controlled by fear. I will not sleep my days away (just to be clear on that last statement — I will still sneak in a nap because naps are amazing, but it's going to be because I want one, not because I NEED one.) This is the year I start living again. Join me. It's gonna be awesome!

PART 4: LOVING

PERSPECTIVE FROM LOVED ONES

*Rape is Just Another Word
until it happens to
your wife,
your daughter,
your sister,
your mother,
your aunt,
your niece,
your cousin,
your best friend,
YOU.
Then it becomes pain you live
with for the rest of your life.*

Author's Note to the writers. I know you all struggled writing your sections for this book. I thank you for your love, your honesty, your support and simply loving me through this. I wouldn't have made it this far on my own.

A Real-Life Nightmare

Henry's Story

I remember weeks before her trip to Sochi, Brenda was nervous about it. The first time she had been to Sochi, her clients accompanied her, and they provided security to escort them around the city. This time around, they were on their own. There would be no security. No one who could translate the language or the street signs or anything. At least she had a female counterpart going on the trip with her, but that didn't bring her much comfort. She was stressed and nervous about going.

I would try to reassure her everything would be ok, but my words fell on deaf ears. I mean, she had been on plenty of trips before. She was always traveling to places such as LA, DC, NYC, Seattle, Boston, London, Beijing, Shanghai, and she had even been to Moscow/Sochi once before. She was a seasoned traveler, what could go wrong?

The first part of the week in Moscow went just fine. We had added an international calling plan to our cell phones, but it was still expensive and only came with 50 texts. If we wanted, 50 texts could happen in a single conversation. As a result, she would only send me texts if it was important. "We landed safely in Moscow, headed to the hotel." Otherwise, we stuck to emailing. She would send me daily emails of what she did and would include pictures. Pictures of the Ritz-Carlton Moscow, the Kremlin, St. Basil Cathedral, and other sights. It seemed like she was getting settled in and everything was fine.

She spent a couple of days in Moscow and then headed to Sochi. They had to take a flight then catch a car to their hotel. The hotel in Sochi was new and was built specifically for the 2014 Winter Olympics. It was so new that the road leading up to the hotel wasn't finished. If getting there was any indication of how this trip was going to go, let's just say it took more than an hour to find a route into the hotel turnaround. Eventually, they made it to the hotel safe and sound.

The trip was not going as planned. The clients weren't happy, and when the clients aren't happy, Brenda's not happy. Add to that the language barriers and dislike for Americans, Brenda and Lynn had a tough trip. In one email, Brenda complained that the police wouldn't let the taxi driver drop them off at the front of the hotel. He made the taxi driver let them out up the road and made her and Lynn walk through a newly tarred and very muddy street to get to the hotel while he laughed at them. Brenda mentioned that from what she could understand between the driver and the policeman, they were made to walk because they were American.

Sochi is nine hours ahead of Chicago Central Standard Time. I remember the day was Saturday and it was a gorgeous fall day outside. Brenda had sent me a note that morning saying that she and Lynn were going to go down to the hotel bar to celebrate making it through the week. She had another week or so left in Russia. She earned it. I told her to have fun and be safe.

PART 4: LOVING

The morning and afternoon went along just fine. Our son, Braeden, had a baseball game and I was the coach. Before we left for the game, I sent a text to Brenda with some sort of pleasantry in it. It was really just to check in. The game started and things were going fine. Braeden was playing nine-year-old fall ball.

During the game, Braeden hit a little league grand slam. With the bases loaded, he hit a ball to right-center field. The field we were playing on didn't have an outfield fence so as the ball kept rolling, Braeden rounded the bases as fast as he could. Braeden isn't an overly fast kid, and this was his first ever home run. This was a big deal for our nine year old son. As he approached home plate, his team was there to congratulate him. It was a proud parent moment that I was fortunate to witness, but I felt bad that Brenda was on the other side of the world and missed it. I texted her right away and told her that her son had not only hit his first home run, but it was a grand slam. No response. That's when I started to get worried.

I was used to certain texting behavior from Brenda. Whether she was at work in Chicago, or on a business trip abroad, I could text her that I was thinking about her and that I loved her and not get a response for a couple of hours. This wasn't a big deal, and I understood. If she was in a meeting, I knew she couldn't always respond right away. But when I texted her something good about the kids, without fail, she would text back immediately. Brenda traveled a lot for work, and her only complaint was that she didn't like missing out on the kids' events and seeing their accomplishments. She always told me how much she appreciated it when I would send updates when something "big" happened, and she would always respond with a message of love and congratulations for the kids.

When Braeden hit his first home run ever, and she didn't respond, that worried me a little bit. As the game wore on, and there was still no response, my worry grew. I remember asking a mom from our team who was really good friends with Brenda at the time if she had heard from Brenda that day. She said no, which was also weird. I know she was limited on her texting, but she would send messages to her friend every now and then.

The game ended and the day went on. As the hours passed, I had still not heard from Brenda, and my concern grew. Like I said, Brenda was nine hours ahead of us. So, around 3PM our time, midnight Sochi time, I sent a text saying something to the effect of, "Just checking in, haven't heard from you in awhile, I hope you're safe and having fun." No response.

Then, "It's 1AM your time, and I'm starting to get worried about you. Are you ok?" No response.

"It's 2AM, and I am really worried. Let me know you are ok." No response.

"It's 3AM your time, and I am freaking out here. Please let me know you're ok." No response.

Logically, I knew there had to be a reasonable explanation why she wasn't responding. Maybe her phone died, or she left it in her room, but it was totally not like her to not respond in some way.

At about 4:15AM Sunday, Sochi time, 7:15PM Saturday Chicago time, I finally receive a text from Brenda. "I just woke up in my room. I think someone put something in my drink. I don't know where my phone is." I just looked at that text and began responding with questions. However many texts she had left on her cell plan just went out the window because I was frantic.

"Are you ok?"

"What happened?"

PART 4: LOVING

"How are you texting me if you don't know where your phone is?"

"Are you ok?"

"Are you ok?"

"Are you ok?"

She was slow to respond. She responded that she was on her iPad, that she doesn't remember anything about the night, felt very unsettled, but she was ok. And it stopped. No more responses.

I kept texting back. "What happened?" "Should I call someone?" "Are you ok?" "Did somebody hurt you?" Nothing. I could imagine the constant buzz of her iPad as I kept sending message after message. But I received no response. What does a man do when his wife is in peril on the other side of the world in a country where nobody speaks your language?

I knew her counterpart's name was Lynn. I didn't know her last name. I knew her boss's name was Tom. I didn't know his last name. I didn't know who to call. At that point, I didn't even know what hotel she was staying at. Then I remembered that Brenda is smarter than me and she had sent me her travel itinerary a couple weeks before. I looked through my emails and found the hotel where she was staying.

I quickly dialed the number, but it didn't work. I had to Google the international code to dial Russia, and it worked. A man answered the hotel phone completely in Russian. I spoke slowly and explained that my wife was a guest in their hotel and that I had received a strange text from her and thought something was wrong. In broken English, I remember him saying that he would check on her and call me back. I repeated my cell phone number twice for him.

In 15 minutes, he called back. There was definitely a language barrier. All I could make out was "She ok. Checked room video. She sleeping." I thanked him and asked him to connect me to her room. He responded, "It's 5AM, you call back at 10 or 11." I told him that I thought something had happened and that he needed to connect me to her room. He repeated, "It's 5AM, you call back at 10 or 11" and click, he hung up on me. I was stunned. I called right back, asked to be connected to her room. I wanted to make sure she was ok. He responded with the same message, "It's 5AM, you call back at 10 or 11" and click, he hung up on me again. I have never experienced anything like that before in my life. I didn't know what was going on and I felt helpless to do anything about it. I sent Brenda more texts pleading with her to please call me. There was silence for hours.

Suffice it to say, I didn't get any sleep that night. I sat and stared at my phone waiting for something to happen. I didn't know who else to call. I still had no clue how to reach her boss or any of her coworkers. Plus, it was now Sunday. I hadn't gotten anywhere with the hotel where she was staying. There was nothing I could do. It wasn't until early morning when the sun was coming up that I finally got a message from her. She said she had passed out and slept since she last reached out to me. She still didn't know where her phone was or what happened. She said she was in pain and couldn't see out of one of her eyes.

I asked her what happened? And she responded in sort of a stream of consciousness way. She really didn't remember what happened last night. Her and Lynn were at the bar. They weren't drinking heavily. Finally, a group of people who she thought were from the UK came into the bar. She was relieved because they all spoke English. These people were contractors who were working on the Olympic venues.

I could see her mood change in the texts. I called her as I wanted to hear her voice but she wouldn't answer. I asked a ton of questions, but most importantly, I asked if someone hurt her. She responded that she was in a lot of pain and that

PART 4: LOVING

she was finding bruises all over her body: On her knees, the back of her legs, her arms, on her chest.

"What happened to you?" I texted. And finally, she responded, "If you want to know if I had sex last night, yes, it feels like I had very rough sex last night." My heart dropped. It's hard to describe the feelings that flooded my body at that moment. Dread, sadness, anger, fear, despair. Then she said, "But I don't know who it was and based on all of these bruises, I never gave consent. I just want to come home."

I told her that we needed to report this right away. That we should call the front desk and report this and/or call the police. She was scared and didn't want to call anyone. She responded that she was in a corrupt third world country and didn't trust anyone, including the police. She was adamant. My hands were tied. What could I do? She told me she had to meet Lynn in the lobby and had a meeting to attend. She still had at least a week left in Russia but wanted to come home. Her administrative assistant was unreachable, so she began making the arrangements to get home herself. I told her to reach out after her meeting.

How does one go about their day after finding out their wife was raped in a foreign country the night before? Our kids were 9 and 11 at the time, and they needed their dad. I still had responsibilities. The task before me was to keep busy without letting the kids know that anything was wrong with their mom. I asked my Mom for help with the kids. I didn't tell my Mom what happened yet as I didn't have the answers, but at least it got the kids out of the house.

When I would talk or text Brenda, every emotion she had came out. Fear, anger, sadness. As she discovered more bruises and felt more pain, the reality of her situation set in. I wanted nothing more than to contact the authorities but she pleaded with me not to. I have to admit, I was conflicted.

Was she telling me the truth? Why wouldn't she want to call the police? But I couldn't come out and question her story.

It was a call with my boss at the time that helped put things into perspective. I told him that I had to work to get her home and he told me to take all the time I needed. He told me that I had to realize that she just experienced a traumatic event, that she was scared and just wanted to get out of the country and come home. Brenda had told me these things too, but it wasn't until an outside person told me the same thing that it sunk in.

Brenda's only request was for me to schedule an appointment with her primary care doctor for when she got home. The earliest flights out of Sochi were on Monday, she'd have to have a layover in Moscow that night, fly to Heathrow early Tuesday AM and that I needed to pick her up late Tuesday afternoon at O'Hare airport. It was still Sunday for me, so I had a little time. My Mom came back with the kids in time for a late afternoon baseball game.

One of my assistant coaches was an Emergency Room doctor at our local hospital. He could sense that something was wrong. Without completely breaking down, I told him what had happened. He said that if we needed anything to let him know. That he could arrange for her to be seen at the ER — he could make some calls to get her right in on Tuesday. I really appreciated that.

Monday came. I couldn't work, and the kids were at school. Brenda was on her way to Moscow for the night before leaving for home. I was stirring like a caged animal. I was mad at not being able to do anything. I felt powerless. My mind was filled with chaos. I felt responsible. How could I let this happen to her? The reality was there was nothing I could do. She told me not to contact anyone — that she just wanted to see her primary care doctor and put this all behind her. End of story.

PART 4: LOVING

I didn't have any experience with a person who had just gone through a sexual assault, but I know Brenda. She is strong willed and focused and, while I knew better than to think she could just put this behind her, she made her wishes clear in no uncertain terms. I knew I wouldn't be able to put this behind me, but what was I supposed to do?

None of this was about me, I got that. I wasn't the one who was raped. I was not the one who had to figure out how to get home and then make that trip in pain. But I was the one who would have to deal with this when she got home. I started to think about things I could do. In my head, my justification was that I was giving her options. I started to take what little control I had, and I called the Geneva Police Department. I vaguely explained the situation and the dispatcher connected me with a detective. I realized he was a local police detective, and this situation was taking place internationally, but I needed his advice on what her options would be once she got home.

Surprisingly, he gave me the number to an FBI agent he worked with on a recent case. The FBI would have access to more resources, so he encouraged me to call him. He did advise that I take her to the emergency room. That if there ever was a case, the legal way was to get a rape kit taken in the ER. If she went to her primary care doctor, they could treat her, but none of it could be used as any kind of evidence. This was good to know.

My next step was to call the FBI agent. I contacted him and left a voicemail. He actually called me back fairly quickly. He was able to connect me to an FBI special agent in charge in Moscow as well as a contact with the US Embassy in Moscow. It was now late in the evening in Moscow, so I called the FBI agent there. He was nice, despite the hour.

Brenda had left Sochi and was almost to Moscow at this point. He wanted to arrange to have her seen in a Moscow hospital and explained that the FBI does not have jurisdiction in Russia. They would act as a middleman representing Brenda. They would have to build a case and present it to the Russian authorities who would then have to take action. I received a call from someone at the US Embassy in Moscow as well. I was still learning about options.

It was the middle of the night Moscow time when I spoke to Brenda over the phone. When I told her what I had done, she was furious with me. She was in pain and scared and reiterated that all she wanted was to come home. It was about midnight where she was. There had been some confusion with the car service, and she was stressed out that it wouldn't be there to pick her and Lynn up at 3AM as planned. She was panicked that she wasn't going to make it home.

She didn't trust anyone at that point. It wasn't up for discussion. She said she would let me know if/when she made it to the airport and would check in when she could. She gave me the time her flight was landing at O'Hare on Tuesday, and that was it. She told me that if she allowed the FBI and Embassy to take her to the hospital, it would prolong her stay, she'd have to reschedule her flight home from Russia and that was not an option.

She mentioned being afraid of the Russian police. The Olympics were a big deal for Russia, and she was afraid that any type of bad PR would result in her being made to disappear. I thought she was irrational at the time, but I wasn't in her shoes. I had to call the FBI agent in Moscow back and let him know she was getting in the car and going to the airport. His concern was that any drug in her system would be gone by the time she made it back to the States. At that point, it was out of my hands.

I was still at home on Monday, and none of this was sitting right with me. I had a wife who was scared and in pain trying to make her way home. I wanted someone to

PART 4: LOVING

pay. Someone needed to be brought to justice for this. I had spoken to the local police, the FBI here in the States and in Russia as well as the US Embassy in Moscow. But there was nothing I could do. At this point, Brenda and Lynn were on the plane to London for their layover.

The Geneva Police Detective I had spoken with called me and asked if I thought Brenda would want to push for a case. I said that I really didn't know. On the one hand, if she was checked out by a doctor and given an ok bill of health, she wouldn't want to do anything. But if she had some type of STD, that would surely piss her off, and she could go on a rampage. He just told me to keep him in the loop.

Next, I called my ER doctor friend. He told me that if Brenda decided she wanted to come to the ER, I should call him. He wasn't working, but he could alert the nurse there to get her into a private room right away. I told him I would keep him in the loop and thanked him.

At some point, I started wondering about security at the hotel where Brenda was staying. This whole event happened in that hotel. It was new, and I remembered the person I spoke to on the phone said something about video. I took a shot in the dark and googled the phone number for the hotel's corporate offices. I spoke to someone in their customer service department and asked about their procedure for obtaining security camera footage in the event of some type of attack. Being that this happened in another country, she didn't know. All she could do was take the note and give it to the General Manager of the hotel in Sochi to review.

I believe it was Tuesday morning when I received a phone call from that General Manager. He wasn't Russian. He had a delightful accent though I couldn't place the country of origin. He expressed his concern and said he had just returned from a meeting at the US Embassy and they were taking this incident very seriously. He wanted to make sure that something like this doesn't happen again in his hotel.

I got the feeling he was speaking out of both sides of his mouth. He said he was concerned and to let him know if we needed anything, but then said to please direct all inquiries to the proper authorities. I later received an email from him stating that they had secured all the video from the evening and started an internal investigation through their Global Security Team. So now we just had to wait to see what happened.

Tuesday came, and I had to go pick up Brenda from the airport. The kids were at school so I asked my Mom if she could get them. I told her what happened but told her not to tell anyone. Brenda didn't want anyone to know that she had been raped. My Mom told me to take care of Brenda and that she and the kids would be at home waiting for us.

I was scared when I pulled into the O'Hare International Terminal parking lot. I didn't know what to expect out of Brenda. How would she look? What would her reaction to me be? I knew this incident would change our relationship, but how? I then received a text from Brenda stating she landed and got through customs quicker than expected. I ran to the doors where she would be coming out. She had her luggage. She was limping and walking slumped over. Her left eye was swollen shut. She wasn't wearing any makeup, and her hair was a mess.

I walked up to her and prepared to take her suitcase and bag from her. Do I touch her? What do I say? We said nothing. She just put her arms around me, buried her head into my chest and started sobbing. I rubbed her back and told her it was ok. That she was safe and no one could hurt her here. After a minute or two, we walked back to the car. I put her in the car and put her luggage in the trunk.

PART 4: LOVING

I was wondering where her co-worker Lynn was, but she had already left. While nothing happened to her in Russia, the event freaked her out. I don't think she handled the situation well. On the one hand, I understood it. What do you say to a person who had been drugged, battered, bruised, and raped? But on the other hand, it didn't even seem like she tried. I digress.

Brenda and I were in the car, still in the airport parking lot, when I updated her on what I had done while she was in the air. I told her we could go see her primary care doctor in the morning or get into the ER tonight but that if she ever wanted to try to bring her rapist to justice, we needed to go to the ER and that the FBI would meet us there. I said I only did it to give her options but would understand whatever option she chose. In my head, I hoped she would choose the ER. And she did. So, I called my doctor friend, and he gave me instruction on where to go and whom to ask for. We then drove home through Chicago rush hour traffic and didn't say much of anything to each other.

When we arrived at the ER, we asked for the nurse, and she came out right away with a wheelchair. Brenda gently sat down, and we went to a private room. The nurse practitioner did the exam. She documented all the bruises on Brenda's body. You could even see a bruise in the form of a handprint on her sternum where the monster that raped her held her down. That someone would touch any person like this let alone my wife was sickening.

But I had to keep calm. I knew that my calm would be her calm, so I bottled it up. They did an examination of her eye and found that her cornea was scratched. They put some drops in her eye which helped. I could tell she was frustrated because she couldn't recall how she got any of these injuries. She also had a lot of pain in her pelvic region and inside of her. I think once they relieved some of the pain in her eye, she calmed down a bit.

The one thing that struck me about the exam was how nice the nurse and staff of the hospital were. They were very caring, and I will be forever grateful for that. They kept us informed the entire way. Since the rape happened four days prior and Brenda eventually showered, they didn't think they would find any DNA evidence, so they didn't even try. They gave her a cocktail of antibiotics and the morning after pill.

I asked whether they would test for STDs and they said no. The reason they gave was that if she tested positive for something, it could be used in court. There would be no way to tell who infected whom. Instead, they gave her a cocktail of antibiotics to cover all of the most common STDs — syphilis, gonorrhea, etc. It made me angry knowing that an attacker could use a disease he gave to a victim against that victim and later sue stating she gave it to him. There are no words.

I then asked about HIV/AIDS. This is where it gets scary. The markers that would indicate HIV wouldn't show up in the body for a good 3-6 months. Brenda would have to go home and wait at least that long to get tested. She would then need to be re-tested at the one year anniversary. That's a long time to wait and wonder if some stranger you don't know or remember gave you a death sentence.

The hospital had called a woman from an organization called Mutual Ground. The advocate explained that they could provide support if Brenda wanted to talk. They also told us her rights as a rape victim in the state of IL. We appreciated that. Then I received a call from our local FBI agents. They were going to try to come to the hospital to take a statement but decided it might be better to come see her at the house the following day. Brenda was still not completely on board with the FBI being involved but agreed she'd be more comfortable talking with them in our home.

PART 4: LOVING

I don't remember much of the night after that. After several hours at the hospital, we got home. The kids were excited to see their mom, but it was their bedtime, so that solved that issue. I put Brenda to bed, and she went to sleep.

Wednesday morning, the FBI came to the house as planned. A bunch of it seemed very stereotypical of what you would think an encounter with the FBI would be like. A male and a female agent got out of a Chevy Tahoe with dark tinted windows. They were both wearing black suits. I answered the door, and they reached into their jackets and pulled out their ID badges. Wow, they really do that. They introduced themselves as Special Agents but said to call them by their first names. My guess was to make them seem more human and personable. We sat down at the dining room table. They asked for my statement and then excused me so they could question Brenda.

In the end, they took the clothes she was wearing that night and said they would be in touch. Brenda was upset because she didn't think they believed her. They asked questions about our relationship. We have had our ups and downs, but we were doing fine. Again, I thought she was just irrational.

Over the course of the next few weeks, Brenda recovered from her physical wounds. The bruises eventually faded. Her eye returned to normal. We had to go to see her primary care physician for a follow-up and then went to see her gynecologist as she was having terrible pain in her pelvic region. She went to the doctor multiple times, as it seemed to take forever for her to heal "down there."

During that time, I had several more conversations with the FBI and the General Manager of the hotel in Sochi. Brenda's case was transferred from the Chicago FBI office to the Washington DC office because they had "more resources." Close to Thanksgiving, I was on my way home from an appointment when

Brenda called me. She was upset. The FBI agent in charge called her on her cell phone and told her that there was no case to be had. The hotel did their own internal review of the videotapes and determined that no crime was witnessed on those tapes. They dropped off the clothes she was wearing the night of the attack, still sealed in the evidence bags they were initially put in. They were never opened.

Since I was in the car, I asked Brenda for the agent's phone number so I could hear for myself what was going on. He told me that all the evidence was circumstantial. The video showed no crime being committed. Testimony from Lynn was that she and Brenda went up to their rooms. Lynn didn't get the sense that anything was wrong though Lynn was intoxicated herself. They were staying on separate floors. Brenda got off on the 2nd floor. She said a man also got onto the elevator but didn't say anything to the women other than to ask which floors they were staying on. Brenda said 2. Lynn said 7. He got off the elevator after Brenda. That was the last she saw of Brenda that night. The FBI agent told me that according to Lynn, when she got off the elevator, Brenda was fine.

But the reality is — things were NOT fine. This angered me greatly. Yes, she was fine when she got off the elevator, but at some point after that, my wife was dragged into a hotel room and raped. She wasn't raped in the hallway. The crime was being committed in the hotel room. Just because it didn't happen on camera doesn't mean a crime wasn't committed.

The FBI agent explained that the FBI is intrusive by nature. For them to bring a case to the Russian authorities, they needed concrete evidence of a crime, and they just didn't have it. I asked why her clothes were never tested. He told me the clothes would have been tested for semen if they could prove a crime took place. Since they couldn't prove the

PART 4: LOVING

crime happened, the bags were never opened. He told me I needed to get past this and move on. He finished by telling me to be careful what I wished for, that I might not like what I found out. I asked him what that was supposed to mean. He didn't expound on that statement.

I told him that I am the one there at night when she wakes up screaming with night terrors; And when she shakes uncontrollably in her sleep; And when she starts crying out of nowhere. I knew my wife was raped and I was getting the sense that the FBI didn't believe her. It seemed to me that he didn't do anything in this case and just like that, it was over. That was her worst fear — to not be believed. Little did I know that this was just the beginning of what was to come.

Brenda slept a lot and, over time, I could see her anxiety manifest. She would get stressed out of nowhere and start yelling. It didn't matter who you were, if you said or did something she didn't like, she would let you know. I'm an adult so I could take it. I drew the line at her yelling at the kids for no reason. For example, we went to Lowes as a family for something small. Within 10 steps of walking in the door, she was yelling at the kids. I don't remember what for, but it was unacceptable. I told her to stop, had her sit down in the lawn furniture section, and I took the kids to get what we needed. Then we left. She never had such a short fuse before. It was frustrating for all of us.

I was fortunate enough to have a job where I could work from home. We got through Christmas and the New Year and Brenda was bored at home. She wanted to regain some semblance of her old life back, so she went back to work. Day one, she drove into the city. I told her to let me know when she arrived at work. She called me from the parking garage. She was terrified and didn't want to get out of the car. "There's a person by the elevator," she told me in a frightened tone. That person got on the elevator and was gone. I told her that no one wanted to hurt her. I would stay on the phone with her until she made it to her office.

She took notice of everyone that passed her on the street. She was hypervigilant. She finally got to her office with some sense of relief. She didn't like riding the elevator. The day seemed to go by without incident, and it was time for her to come home. She called me to tell me she was headed back to the parking garage. She called me when she got to her car, and I said I would see her when she got home. About an hour and a half later, I was getting nervous because she wasn't home yet.

My phone rang, it was Brenda. She was confused. She asked me if she was supposed to go on a trip. I said, "No, why?" She said, "I'm at O'Hare driving around. Are you sure I'm not supposed to go on a trip? I'm not supposed to go to Boston, am I?" "No, you aren't supposed to go to Boston," I said. As confused as she was, I really didn't know what to make of this. At first, I thought she was joking. She said she didn't know how she got there. She remembered driving out of the parking garage and then she remembered being at O'Hare. She was starting to freak out, so I had to keep her calm. I didn't know where she was exactly so I couldn't help her get home. I said that she needed to hang up with me, turn on the GPS on her phone, type in home and let it guide her from there. She didn't want to hang up, but I didn't know what else to do. An hour later she arrived home very shaken.

We made an appointment first thing in the morning with her therapist. She described this as what's called a "fugue state" which she said was like a temporary amnesia. This wasn't the last fugue state she would have. She's driven to Milwaukee on her way to work; A mall nowhere close to our house and gotten frozen yogurt; A cemetery a few towns over and to a forest preserve — but not before stopping for

PART 4: LOVING

some Dairy Queen which she doesn't remember eating. Each time, I have had to help her come out of the fugue state and get home. It was hard because I didn't, and still don't, know what triggers them.

There would be times when we were sitting on the couch watching TV. You would be surprised at how much rape content is on TV when you are sensitive to it. Law and Order, Chicago PD, Grey's Anatomy, Reign, Scandal, the local news…the list goes on. When something comes on that is questionable, I pause the TV and ask her if she is ok to watch it. Most times she says she is ok.

Many times, we will be watching TV, and there is nothing bad on. We will be talking, and I'll look over, and she is staring into space, with a blank look on her face. At first, I took offense, as she had never done this before. I would call her name, and she would not respond. I would talk louder and nothing. Finally, I would let out a loud clap, and she would come out of it in a panic. I was standing right in front of her when it happened, she was looking right at me when I clapped so why was she so freaked out? I didn't understand it.

At work, her company was in the process of moving offices. Her team was the last to move, so for 1-2 weeks, she was on an empty floor with only a bunch of movers. She would stay in her office, lock the door, and then call me freaking out. I didn't know what to tell her. I even volunteered to come to her office and stay with her. She would go to meetings and space out, not being able to recall what she had been saying. She would come home and cry telling me that she wanted to do well at work but she wasn't able to give her clients the kind of attention they were accustomed to from her.

Everyone who knew her situation at work was very nice to her, but it came to the point that she and her bosses agreed she needed to go back on leave until she could fully heal. I believe this was in the April timeframe. She took this hard. She wanted to be better. The reality was that this was another setback for her.

Brenda would go see her therapist on a weekly basis. It took a while for her to warm up to her. On the one hand, she desperately wanted help, but on the other hand, Brenda had spent 15+ years working in an industry where she was trained not to show her feelings. To say she has a tough time talking about them is the understatement of the year.

Eventually, she grew to trust this therapist, but then it was suggested she try a different type of therapy — EMDR. I have no clue what it stands for, but she had to switch therapists. Her new therapist's name was Suzanne. Brenda had a rough time with the transition and would often refer to her new therapist as the voodoo witch doctor. It took time, but they now have a great relationship, and Brenda seems to be getting a lot out of these appointments.

In the meantime, she also started seeing a psychiatrist because her primary care doctor was past her point of comfort in treating her when the fugue states started. Dr. Shea is a good man who worked out of a local hospital. However, it was a six-week wait for a new patient appointment. Once she started seeing him on a regular basis, she quickly became at ease with him. Dr. Shea eventually left that practice to venture out on his own. His new office was on Michigan Ave in the heart of downtown Chicago. Every trip was full of triggers for Brenda.

Again, I was fortunate to have a job that allowed me to work out of the house. I was always there when Brenda needed me. There were/are days when she will sleep the entire day. She won't shower, she won't put on normal clothes. She will stay in her pajamas, and if she needs anything, she will send me a text, and I will bring it to her. The doctor diagnosed her

PART 4: LOVING

with PTSD. I thought only people fighting wars get PTSD. No, Brenda was broken.

Brenda still spaces out or dissociates, a lot. I sat in on a therapy session once, and Suzanne gave me tips on how to pull Brenda out of a dissociative state. I wasn't to clap, yell, or make loud noises. Brenda isn't aware she is doing it. She is escaping into her mind in response to some type of stimuli. Again, I have no clue what the trigger is. I am supposed to kneel down next to her and nudge her gently until she comes to. I then have to make sure she feels safe and grounded. I tell her to look left and then right. Take notice of her surroundings. This typically does the trick.

I have never asked Brenda about her attack. I don't know what she remembers and what she doesn't. Right after my final conversation with the FBI agent, I sent the general manager of the hotel a message. He called me the next day. He was nice, but his tone changed. He knew there was no case. He told me the local authorities never contacted him because the FBI never contacted them. He not only worked for the parent company of the hotel, but he also worked for the franchise owner who owned that particular hotel in Sochi.

I said I wasn't interested in a name. What I wanted to know was the timeline. What happened and when? He said that he couldn't tell me anything. That he didn't even know if I was who I said I was. We had talked on several occasions and exchanged numerous emails and NOW he is questioning my identity? He said he knew what Brenda looked like from her passport photo on file and he would talk to her on Skype. I told him I would check with Brenda and get back to him.

I talked to Brenda; she wanted me to come to a therapy session with her, and we could talk about it with Suzanne. Suzanne asked me what I wanted to gain from this. I really didn't have a clue. I just wanted to know, I didn't know why. I was angry, and I wanted clarity. Suzanne confirmed that Brenda still has no memory and that might be a saving grace. It could be much harder if Brenda could remember a face, a name, or details of the rape. She thought it was better if I left it alone. Personally, I was tired of leaving things alone, but I complied. Nothing ever happened with the case after that.

PTSD is terrifying. Not just for the person who has it, but also for the people around to witness it. Brenda goes to sleep at night and vibrates. She shakes a lot. It's like her anxiety is a physical person in the room. It transfers to me, and I can't fall asleep. There have been a few instances where I am able to fall asleep, only to be woken up by a slap or punch to the face or a kick to the body. Brenda will have a night terror and attack me. "No!" She'll scream. I will work to calm her down till she falls back asleep. Then I'll move further away from her in bed or go sleep on the couch. She'll wake up in the morning and say how exhausted she is because she didn't sleep at night, so she has to go back to sleep.

Other symptoms? Night sweats? Yeah, she has those. If I go to put my arm around her, she is covered in sweat. A pool of it. Gross. Talking in her sleep? Yeah, she does that too. It's usually her mumbling, "Please don't hurt me." "Please don't, I'm married," or just pleading "No" in her sleep. I feel horrible when this happens, and again, I talk to her and tell her she is safe, she is loved and no one will hurt her ever again. She will then say thank you but slip right back into her dream and ask me not to hurt her.

Brenda will go through phases. She takes a lot of medication: Antidepressants, antipsychotics, sleeping pills, blood pressure meds, and the list goes on. It's always a test to see what drugs will work. She and Dr. Shea will assess the new side effects and change the dose or try a new drug. If she can't sleep at night, they try a new drug, but then she has

PART 4: LOVING

really bad dreams. Then they try another drug to hopefully suppress the dreams, but it makes her tired, and now she sleeps all day too. Try a different dose. Doesn't work. Switches medications. Try again. It's never ending.

She may go through a period of time where she will string together some good days. She will still take naps, but she will go exercise. A lot. Then she feels good about herself because she is exercising. Then something will happen where she is full of anxiety. She will go to the store and have a panic attack, and that one panic attack will send her into a tailspin.

In the beginning, she had more bad days than good. Every day was full of panic. Eventually, with the help of medication and a lot of therapy, she started having good days. It has always been my job to let her know that it's ok to have bad days. We all have bad days. But with Brenda, a bad day is extreme. She will say things like, "I thought I was getting better." "You are getting better!" I'll tell her.

I don't know much, but I do know baseball, so I'll throw out the only analogy I can think of — when you strike out, that's ok, but it doesn't mean you quit. You have to go back up to the plate and take another at-bat. I don't think it always sinks in when I tell her. After that, she will go through a stretch where she stays in bed all day again. It goes from good to bad to ok to bad to better. It's just hard.

I know she feels bad. She feels bad for how this affects the kids and me. The kids know something happened to her, but only Makena knows the details. I try to shield them from as much as I can. I try to shield Brenda as much as I can. I try to handle all the insurance stuff. Between workman's comp, long term disability, social security disability, Medicare, and attorneys, there's a lot to handle. It can be daunting to deal with and can completely exacerbate her anxiety, so I handle it.

It hasn't been all bad though. I am able to take the kids to school and pick them up. I've never missed a baseball game or practice. But sometimes it can be a bit much. When she has weeks where she is in bed and doesn't leave the bedroom, I am responsible for making sure the kids are fed, and everyone has what they need. I don't complain though. My job is to love her for better or worse; in sickness and in health. I am here for her no matter what.

That is my life now. Wherever we go, whatever we do, I have to plan and be aware of our surroundings. I have to be aware of Brenda's anxiety and mood because anything can set her off. I have to be prepared to calm her down when she feels like her anxiety is out of control. This may involve asking for special rooms at hotels or for tables in quieter areas of restaurants. I don't park near big trucks or vans because those scare her. We used to go to concerts, movies, comedy clubs, but we don't do that anymore. We used to go on quick weekend getaways, but we don't do that anymore. I feel bad writing this because I feel as if this is coming off as complaining. I'm really not complaining. This is just my life.

One question I have gotten from the beginning is, "What are you doing for help?" My response is that I will get help after Brenda is better. I have seen a therapist, but I don't think I've found the right one. I think I am pretty intuitive and can give great advice. I have seen enough to know what is bothering Brenda or if something has triggered her anxiety. Most times I stay quiet and try to help. There are times when I fight back. Sometimes I can see that Brenda is picking a fight. I can tell because everything I say is misconstrued or bothers her. If she sees me getting upset, then she gets upset and says she understands if I want to leave her. I'm not going anywhere.

I have to remind her that I am entitled to feel upset. It's okay for me to feel frustrated. I have bad days just like her. I get depressed and anxious too. The thing is that I don't have the luxury to let that slow me down. The kids still need

PART 4: LOVING

to eat. I still have to work. At times, I get resentful and feel as if I'm not allowed to get upset or feel frustration. I don't like seeing her like this. It has been four years since her rape. Why is she not better yet? But it's not that simple. She is broken. This is like a disease. I constantly try to remind myself that something was taken from her and this will affect her, or I should say us, for the rest of our lives. It's not easy.

How to Hire a Hitman

Kelly's Story

I actually Googled, "How to hire a hitman in Sochi, Russia." It was like any other Sunday morning, lazy and slow. I rolled over in bed, kissed my husband, Tom, and started to get up, begrudgingly. As I sat up, I reached for my phone. That's when I realized I had messages, several of them. I put on my glasses and opened my Facebook Messenger.

What? No! Fear, anger, helplessness, more anger, and overwhelming sadness washed over me instantly. I was reading what had to be a very twisted joke, but there was no punchline, none. It wasn't funny. My best friend, my sister, was half way around the world, and she needed me.

I sprung out of bed and began dressing. Tom, my husband, woke confused. He asked me, "Who died? What's wrong? Where are you going?" I couldn't answer through the flood of emotions. Honestly, I didn't know who was going to die (anger), what was wrong (helplessness), or where I was going (fear and more anger). All I knew was I needed to be with Brenda, and now. How far away is Sochi, anyway (sadness)?

PART 4: LOVING

I ran downstairs and opened our chat on my laptop. I began looking for a way to get to her. There was no way. I would need a passport and a visa. Both of which would take far too long. Dammit! Google, "How to hire a hitman in Sochi, Russia?" In hindsight, I was leaving an electronic trail, but I didn't give a flying fuck.

I had no money, no time, and I needed to get to her. You see, that's my job. It always has been. In the thirty-odd years that we've known each other, she has been the leader, and I have been the rock behind her so she couldn't stumble backward as she forged our future. Yes, our future. Whether intentional, or not, she has been the pioneer of this sisterhood, and I follow, as the clean-up crew. For example, she played clarinet, and a few years later, I played the clarinet. She went to college, and a few years later, I went to the same college. I've always found comfort in following her. That's one of the best parts about having a best friend who is older than you, right? There is something to be said about knowing she survived a life decision that made me confident. I owe everything to her adventurous, pioneering self.

She is my strong, path-carving, professional, beautiful, smart, Type-A friend. She is a survivor, proven time and again. We've been through so much together. Really, she has been through so much, and I inserted myself as her crutch, the rock. When we were young, her brother and I were actually closer friends. I was very much a rough and tumble tomboy. Jason and I played outside, rode dirt bikes, and climbed trees. I can't tell you how old I was when Brenda and I really started to hang out; I don't remember. I'm sure it started with her conning me into cleaning her room and giving me some silly treasure as a reward. Maybe she even let me play with that doll of hers that I coveted so much. (In hindsight, that was the ugliest doll, ever. Receding hairline. That one blinky eye that always seemed to get stuck. She was creepy.

Sorry, Brenda.) Anyway, who knows when the connection happened, but eventually she couldn't shake this little girl with brown eyes, long knotty brown hair, and dirty bare feet. If you are seeing some Norman Rockwell girl, try again.

While I am certain our childhoods were far from picturesque, they were pretty amazing. We had room to run, friends to play with, and families who watched out for us all. In 1989, our first major tragedy struck. Brenda and Jason's dad died, suddenly, at 38 years old. I am sad to say that somehow, I knew before they did. In fact, when they were brought home from their grandparents' house, I was there. I sat on the bed next to Brenda, young and unsure how to be her rock. I was 11.

In 1995, her mom passed after a tough battle with cancer. Again, I wanted to be with her, and was. In fact, this is the 'rock' that went back to her house, alone, and fished "more comfortable" shoes from her closet during the wake because the shoes she chose to wear that day were cute but impractical (shocking.) I was scared to death walking into the house of a dead woman, but it was my job.

Brenda got married when I was twenty, and I was there doing snow angles on the floor in my Maid of Honor dress, which I hated, but never told her, until now. I got married, and she was there by my side, and it was perfect. We had our first babies four months apart, and it was perfect. We both had our second babies, and it was perfect. I started to believe that we were through the hardest times. I was wrong.

Losing both parents was hard for both Brenda and Jason. At the time, it seemed to have a larger impact on Jason. His then girlfriend was pregnant when his mom passed away. Jason still hadn't recovered from the loss of his dad. He spiraled out of control, and the girlfriend and his infant son went their own way. While heartbreaking, it was for the best. Even Jason could recognize his demons. The years of anger

PART 4: LOVING

and sorrow lead him to booze and drugs, most of which he successfully hid from those of us that cared about him the most. Then one day in July of 2004, he finally snapped. His life came undone, his then wife headed for the hills with their newborn daughter, and he wound up in a rehab facility. It was horrible and heartbreaking. It was then that I realized the hard times wouldn't stay away.

Our focus remained on Jason for a long time. Aunts, uncles, and grandparents passed, Jason continued to have his difficulties. All Brenda and I could do was pray and support. It's sad to say that we found such comfort in him getting a bit portly. That meant he wasn't doing drugs. Winning! He met a girl and married her. He was happy. Another win. Comfort began to creep up on us again. The worst was over, just maybe.

Until that fateful Sunday morning, we were winning. Until the day that some bastard stole my best friend's confidence. Until the moment when my heart broke, again. I couldn't fix this, I couldn't be with her, I couldn't…imagine. How could I have thought she had been joking, if even for a moment? I wish she had been joking.

All I could do was google home remedies for her injuries. Really, that's all I could do? Yes, that and cry, big, ugly tears. I wanted, no, needed to be with her. I needed to know she was alive. She was sending messages to me, she had to be alive, right? Once I knew she was home, I called off work, and drove the hour and a half to her house, just to touch her. Could I touch her? I didn't want to cause her any more pain. I had to, at least, see her with my own eyes.

As soon as I laid eyes on her, I knew things had changed. How can a heart break so many times and still beat? I gently wrapped my arms around her and cried. She didn't say much. She looked awful, she never looked awful. She looked weak and tired. I had never seen her look that way. I was scared. We talked about if, how, and when she would tell her brother and her Aunt Susan, who had stepped up to fill her mom's shoes. I promised to be with her if she wanted me to.

I didn't know if I did the right thing by going to her house that day. I didn't stay long, although I never wanted to leave her side again. To this day, I am sorry that I didn't just bring my PJs with and stay with her. I found comfort in knowing that her husband, Henry, was there. I worried about her, the kids, and Henry too.

The day came when Brenda decided to tell Aunt Susan. I met her at Aunt Susan's house, and Susan knew something was wrong. Brenda's body language said it all. Brenda and I worked together to tell her. We all cried, and hugged. Maybe they needed to be alone, but I couldn't leave Brenda with anyone. Hell, I barely trusted her husband with her. I was crazy and over protective. I think I still am.

Then one day, Brenda was brave. No, Brenda was brave every day, even when she didn't know she was brave but she told her brother and, in my eyes, this took a whole different level of brave. I wasn't there. I was and still am so proud of her for telling him. He needed to know. She needed him to know. I needed him to know. The more people who knew, the larger Brenda's support system grew. I found comfort in knowing that I was not the only one, "back home," who knew. Hell, in many ways, I needed their support too.

Now I'll tell you about how selfish I am. Once the initial shock of what happened to Brenda began to wear off (it'll never wear off, who am I kidding), I went through a lot of emotions which included anger and frustration toward Brenda. I am as shocked to write this as I am sure she will be to learn of it. I don't believe I ever let on how angry and frustrated I was. I believe it was my own way of processing the time and events (really, "events" what word or words do I use to describe everything that happened during this time…?)

PART 4: LOVING

I went through many of the classic stages of grieving. Yes, I was angry that it happened, but how could I be angry at her, and why? I still don't know, and I may never know. I wanted her to stop sleeping all the time and answer her damned phone when I called. She wasn't the same, and I wanted answers. How long before she was back to normal? Then I became sad, I mourned her. Maybe this was the new normal, but part of her was gone. Did I still love her the same? Yes, absolutely, but was she still my best friend and sister? Did she still like me and want me in her new life? Would we find common ground again? Could we find a way to hang out that didn't require her going to a bar, concert, or out in public? Bottom line, I was scared that some British, piece of ass-twat, had stolen my best friend from me. See, I told you I was selfish. I felt like an ass-twat myself.

Everything I was feeling was changed in a moment on December 13, 2013. I was in a horrible car accident. Sure, I had been in my fair share of car accidents/fender benders, but this was different. I was broadsided at an intersection, less than a mile from my home. I saw the other car coming, sped up to avoid him hitting my passenger door, which may have saved me more serious injury, and was rolled into a deep ditch. The accident left me car-less, scared, bruised, and stole my confidence. I was diagnosed with PTSD and put on medication to help with the nightmares and anxiety. I believe that accident had a purpose. I could now relate to Brenda's anxiety, diagnosis, and medication, if even on a small scale. Prior to my accident, I didn't have a clue. I thought I did, but damn was I stupid!

Once again, Brenda lead, and I followed. I can't imagine why or how, but God intends for us to be together. My selfish, ignorant, ways were tearing us apart, and that needed to change. It did. I grew more patient with her not answering the phone or a text. I learned new ways to connect with her. I found new aspects of Brenda to adore and cherish.

I am thankful for every moment that I have with her. We don't need to go to the bar or a concert to have fun. We don't even have to leave the house to enjoy one another. It's a new friendship. We are new women. It's amazing! She is forever my sister, my best friend. Our bond has grown even stronger. Together, we are self-proclaimed, funny bitches. Seriously, her next book should be dedicated to the hilarity of some of our late-night text sessions. I never thought I'd want to wake up and read texts from Brenda, ever again, but re-reading a series of texts between two, life-long friends, who are high on "night-night" meds is AMAZING!

We are adapting, evolving and we joke about writing each other's eulogies for fun. (I mean, wouldn't you want to know what your best friend thought of you BEFORE you died? I want to be around to hear it!) Okay, so maybe this friendship has it's weird and dark moments. I like to believe it makes us closer and stronger. Our friendship has withstood more than most, and who said there are rules?

I will never again assume the worst is behind us. I will always believe there is more to come. When the more does come, we will be together. Until one day, when we are not. That one day almost happened to us twice. Lord, please, let us be together for a very long time. We have children to raise, husbands to drive crazy, grandchildren to hold, nursing homes to terrorize, and we need each other. She is the pioneer, and I am her rock. I hate the Olympics.

PS – For the record, I did NOT actually hire a hitman. (Brenda thought I needed a legal disclaimer here.)

Wait...Mom was Raped?

Makena's Story

Author's note: my daughter Makena is 15 years old and one of the people I cherish most in this world. I thought it was important she know what happened. When we sat down to talk about it, she was entering high school, starting to venture out more on her own and making her own choices. She was also planning on traveling abroad. I needed to have a conversation about choices, awareness, and safety planning. It was a good discussion. If you have a young woman in your life, please open up the discussion on rape. Let her know that she and her friends can come to you. Talk about what to do and what not to do if it does happen and reiterate that this is NEVER a woman's fault. Empowering and educating our young women is essential if we want to change the conversation about rape from one of taboo to one of survival. I applaud her bravery for opening up the subject and thank God every day for blessing me with such a wonderful daughter. This is her story:

I am told that I was 11 years old when my mom was in Russia. I don't really remember much about her trip or her coming home early. She traveled all the time, so this trip wasn't any different to me. What I knew was that she stopped going to work. At first, she said it was because she had been traveling so much and wanted to spend some time at home with us. Then we learned about her anxiety. Then my Mom told me what happened to her a few months ago. I was 14.

Not only has my mom changed from this, but my whole life has. Before she used to work long weeks, I would barely see her at all, and now she is home with us all day. I love having my mom home, but I do miss going into the city to work with her. I loved hanging out in her office and getting grilled cheese and ice cream from the cafeteria. Having my mom home has changed me so much because I have grown so much closer to her.

Lately, my mom has been looking for new and alternative ways to manage her anxiety. One new thing she is trying is meditating. I think it is a little weird, but I have never been one who likes yoga or can concentrate on being calm. Sometimes it gets hard to be patient with her anxiety issues. I guess that is because I can't really understand what she went through. Some of her medicines make her sleep all day, and I don't understand why. She can get really anxious sometimes, and it will hold us back from going out or doing things. It can be hard to be patient. Before she told me she was raped, I never really thought about what happened because I didn't know. I just went along with it as best as I could.

After finding out what happened, I was scared, confused and mad. It is a hard thing to accept. I think that it is important to know about these things and it makes me mad when I hear kids making jokes about rape. What they don't realize is that it is a very real thing and is not funny to joke about. As of now, my brother doesn't know what happened, but I wish he did. I think it would be good to talk to him

PART 4: LOVING

about it, but I cannot imagine how he would take the news. He just turned 13.

What I can learn from this, and I hope my friends can too, is that there are bad people in the world and bad things can happen to good people. I'm traveling to France with school next week, and I know my Mom is having a hard time letting me go. At the same time, she doesn't want what happened to her to stop me from living my life. I appreciate her concern for my safety, and I really appreciate her bravery for putting her own issues aside and letting me explore the world. Moving forward I will learn from this experience by being aware of my surroundings, whether I am at a party, out with friends or traveling. If it can happen to my Mom, I suppose it can happen to anyone.

Knowing Brenda

Kim's Story

It's hard to know where to start, so I suppose I'll just start in the beginning. I met Brenda in the first few days of college at Valparaiso University. We were assigned to the same dorm floor — Lankenau 2N. My first memories of Brenda were her penchant for drinking whole milk and her entourage of cowboy hat and boot wearing hometown friends. Brenda was more than a "little bit country"...she was a bona fide country girl. As with most college freshman, we were all thrown together for our first tastes of freedom, breaking out of our comfort zones, and meeting new people.

Brenda's personality filled any room she was in, and I remember being drawn to that energy — my more reserved, wait-until-I-get-to-know-you personality, going along for the ride in the wake of her excitement to meet new people and try new things. Brenda was the life of the party, and if there was no party, well then, she made the party herself. And so it began, a friendship born from a random dorm assignment and nurtured by shared college experiences.

Brenda and I shared a similar driven, Type-A approach to college life — study hard, party harder. And we shared a similar no-nonsense, tell-it-like-is approach to life and

PART 4: LOVING

friendships. It could be abrasive to some, and it wasn't warm and fuzzy, but it was real and sincere, and it was and remains a bond between us. We pledged the same sorority, and although we quickly agreed that the "sisterhood" concept wasn't necessarily a good fit for us, we appreciated the social aspect and begrudgingly muddled through the contrived formalities of candle ceremonies and mandatory meetings.

Some of those mandatory meetings included lectures on cliché topics like the risks of binge drinking/alcohol abuse and lessons in personal safety when out at fraternity parties. The irony was not lost on us then, or even when we reminisce now, that we attended many of those meetings while drinking 7-11 Slurpees secretly (and heavily) spiked with Dark Eyes vodka. Nonetheless, we attended the lectures, and we heeded the warnings. Kind of. We traveled in packs down on Mound Street (i.e. fraternity row), we never left a friend behind, and we used the university van to drive us back to our dorm after a night out. We weren't naïve — we knew "bad" things could happen. Indeed, we knew "bad" things did happen. But we were smart, we were strong. We knew what to do and what not to do even if we hadn't paid particularly close (or sober) attention to the lectures. We would be fine.

In our senior year, Brenda and I moved out of the dorms and rented a townhouse with some of other of our Lankenau 2N friends. By that point, we had moved on from our sorority involvement and were excitedly beginning the transition into the next stages of our lives. I had graduated a semester early and was leisurely taking a few graduate classes while Brenda was finishing up her senior year classes. Life in the townhouse was an unmitigated blast, and we were cruising towards the beginning of the rest of our lives with memories and laughs to last a lifetime. For me, that meant heading off to law school, and for Brenda, that meant starting her career in advertising. The bona fide country girl was ready to take on the big city (Chicago) and the world of advertising by storm.

While it was hard to leave our college bubble behind, we left Valpo confident. Confident that we were equipped to face the world head on and achieve our goals. Confident that we had learned what we needed to learn and were ready to put that knowledge into practice. And confident that our friendships would last us the rest of our lives, wherever those lives took us.

After graduation, I moved to Champaign-Urbana, Illinois for law school and Brenda (with Hank—aka Henry—in tow) moved back to the double-wide trailer on her family's farm in Crete, Illinois. But Brenda's drive and ambition were bigger than the double-wide or Crete, and she forged ahead with a daily commute of automobiles, trains, buses, and water taxis to her advertising job in the city. To the surprise of no one that knows her, Brenda's professional star was quickly on the rise.

In an era before the instant communication of text messaging and social media, Brenda and I didn't talk every day like we did during our time at Valpo, but we kept in touch by phone and email, and visits when we could. Time passed. I graduated from law school and moved to Cleveland to start my legal career as an associate lawyer at a large national law firm, and Brenda kept moving up the corporate ladder at her advertising job.

More time passed. We kept in touch with phone calls during our commutes and had dinner together pretty regularly. Well, by dinner together, I mean that since my commute was only about 15 minutes, and Brenda's was well over an hour, I would get home, make, eat, and clean-up my dinner, all while we were still on the phone. It drove her nuts, but

PART 4: LOVING

she still took my commute-time phone calls. Our friendship sustained.

Brenda and Hank got married, moved from the country to the burbs, and had two beautiful children. We were officially adulting. We got together for visits when we could, but life got busy, and visits got harder and harder to come by. But our Valpo friendships with our Lankenau 2N crew were important to us, and we made a concerted effort to make sure we got together at least twice a year — once with our respective families (dubbed our "Valpo Christmas") and once "just the girls". And when life got really, really busy with careers and families, and one too many of our Valpo Christmases resulted in treacherous snowbound travel, we still held tight to our annual girls' weekends. A tradition was born, and, without fail, our Lankenau 2N group met in Florida for a long weekend every April. We all treasured those visits to keep us connected and guarded them fiercely in our respective schedules.

As the years passed, each of our careers advanced and progressed. We commiserated about office politics, exhausting schedules, unreasonably demanding clients, and the blasted billable hour. By this point, Brenda was a senior executive, in charge of her own team of underlings and managing multi-million-dollar advertising budgets for Fortune 500 companies. Brenda had made it. Country girl no more, Brenda was a bonafide power broker in the world of advertising.

Make no mistake, Brenda's job was taxing, but it definitely had its perks. While I was toiling away day after day buried in motion practice and dealing with contentious opposing counsel, Brenda's "work" often included spa treatments, fancy dinners, sporting events and, on occasion, even college-inspired pub crawls masked as "relationship-building". Turns out, Brenda was still the life of the party. Not surprisingly, that same effusive energy that drew a crowd to her in college, myself included, made friends out of perfect strangers when she was traveling the country (and, indeed the world) for her job.

Then came THE assignment — Sochi, Russia ahead of the 2014 Winter Olympics to scope out advertising opportunities for one of her biggest, and most demanding, clients. Just a few years earlier she had successfully placed advertising at the 2012 Summer Olympics in London, so she was up for the challenge and the adventure.

I remember talking to Brenda shortly before she left for Sochi. A few months earlier we had decided to motivate each other to take on the challenge (at least for us) of running our first 5K race, and the race was scheduled for the month after she returned from Sochi. We talked about our mutual disdain for running, our ill-will towards those that boasted of the elusive "runner's high", and our intention to "party like rockstars" when we finished it. Only now, more than a few years removed from our Valpo days, our idea of "partying like rock stars" was less copious amounts of Dark Eyes vodka into the wee hours of the night, and more sitting around in comfy clothes, chatting for hours and indulging in a sweet treat or ten. Our conversation was not particularly significant, and yet, to this day, I remember it. It has become the demarcation in a time of the "before Brenda" and the "after Brenda". Before Sochi. And after Sochi. I miss my friend, "before Brenda", but I'm inspired by my friend, "after Brenda".

While Brenda was in Sochi, we exchanged several emails, and it was clear that the business side of things was not going smoothly. Brenda was experiencing firsthand what the national news outlets would report a few months later when the Olympics opened: Sochi was woefully unprepared and behind schedule in their infrastructure construction and preparation.

PART 4: LOVING

Then there was the "unique" way that business was conducted there...and by "unique", I mean, corrupt. Brenda was finding it impossible to identify and secure prominent and prestigious ad placement opportunities that could be verified with visual, "feet-on-the-ground" confirmation (because things weren't finished being built yet), and even verifiable opportunities couldn't be "secured" without capitulating to nefarious handshake deals and paid-off promises, neither of which were viable options to justify devoting millions of dollars of an advertising budget. It was discouraging, but not defeating. I remember at one point in our email exchange, I told Brenda to "hang in there," that she only had a few days left and she would be on her way back home with our 5k fun awaiting.

And then I got the email. It was 1:12 p.m. EST, and I happened to be sitting at my desk when the email popped up. The subject line read: "Russia gone wrong." Naturally, I opened the email expecting an update on the trials and tribulations of trying to walk the impossible line between identifying and securing an impactful advertising opportunity for her demanding client and ethically and legitimately securing that opportunity in the no-holds-barred business climate of Sochi. It was not that update. At all.

The first line of the email took my breath away. "So, this is the last email you'll ever want to get and trust me, not one I'd ever thought I'd send. I was drugged and raped in my hotel in Sochi." With my heart racing, I frantically read the rest of the email. And then I reread the email again. And again. I just couldn't process the information Brenda was conveying to me. She was hurt. My friend was hurt. Physically battered and bruised. And violated, in the truest most basic sense of the word. And she was in Russia!

How could this be? How did we get from a professional setback (not nailing down the perfect, albeit elusive, advertising opportunity) to a life-threatening (and, as time would show, and as Brenda details in this book, life-altering) crime perpetrated against her? Two very specific memories I still have of reading Brenda's email: first, the surreal feeling of time standing still — all other noise and activity around me ceased to exist as my brain tried to both process the information and process what I needed to do. And second, I had started to cry.

Within minutes of reading and processing Brenda's email, I picked up the phone, and without a second thought to time zones or international cell phone rates, I called Brenda on her cell phone. I willed her to answer — I needed to hear her voice. She did. Her voice was weak, and the physical pain she was in was palpable, but it was her nonetheless, and I was relieved. Hearing her voice, and knowing that she was "ok" — in the sense that she was out of imminent danger or threat from whoever did this to her — allowed my brain to shift into my problem-solving, matter-of-fact lawyer mode.

Where was she now? Moscow, at the Ritz Carlton hotel, waiting on a plane to London.

Was her co-worker physically with her? No, she had another hotel room, but the rooms were close, and they would be traveling to London (and home to Chicago) together.

Did she call the police? No, Sochi was too corrupt, she was scared and hurt, and just wanted to get home.

Had she seen a doctor? No, not there, but Hank had an appointment scheduled for her as soon as she got back home.

What could I do to help her? At that moment, the stark reality for a Type-A problem solver like me was nothing.

The bottom line was Brenda, battered and bruised, alone (except for a co-worker) and scared, still had two international flights and a layover in London ahead of her before she could physically get to those that would love and protect her.

PART 4: LOVING

We talked for a bit, I struggled to find the right words to convey my thoughts of encouragement and strength. Although sincere and heartfelt, in hindsight I often wonder if they felt like hollow platitudes to Brenda at the moment, but she promised to keep me apprised of each step of her journey home.

We hung up, and I remember being at a complete loss of what to do next. It seemed impossible, and almost insulting, to try a go back to "business as usual". Through tears, I sent Brenda an email:

"I know we just hung up, but I can't stop thinking about you. My heart aches for you, and I wish so badly that I could be there for you right now. But you are one of the strongest, bravest, most determined people I know, and I know that this wasn't your fault, and this doesn't define you in any way. The bruises will heal, your heart and psyche will heal, and you will go on. I know. Truly. I know. If you need me — whenever, wherever — I will be there. Stay strong and focus on getting home where you will be safe and loved unconditionally by those two beautiful kids of yours. I love you, dear friend."

I wanted her to know what I had struggled to say over the phone. I wanted her to know that even in the despair and hurt of what at happened, her inner strength and perseverance would pull her through, and that, until then, she had a network of support to lift and hold her up.

My next call was to Hank. We shared information from our respective conversations with Brenda trying to piece together what had happened, what her travel schedule home was, and what we could do to help her when she got there. Brenda arrived home on a Tuesday afternoon. Hank picked her up at the airport and took her to the ER. Brenda's physical injuries were, for the first time, being assessed and treated. I was relieved but still felt helpless.

Although Hank kept me informed, I felt an overwhelming need to see her with my own eyes, to be there for her. (Or was it for me?) I coordinated schedules with Hank, he agreed to shuttle me to and from the airport, and I booked a flight to Chicago. I texted Brenda and told her I planned to see her that Saturday to make sure she was ok with a visit. She responded that she would love to see me but assured me that I didn't need to come, that she wasn't "very good company right now". I told her I wasn't looking for "good company," that I just wanted to see her, to "be there".

When I saw Brenda for the first time, the thing that startled me the most were not the visible cuts and bruises, but her eyes. They were empty and distant. She was happy to see me, and we hugged (lightly, so as to not hurt her bruised body), but there was something vacant about her eyes. It was as if she would muster all her energy for a few moments to really look at me and engage, but then it just was all too exhausting, and her eyes would grow distant, and I could just feel her retreat into herself.

We spent the first few hours sitting in her front living room, and while we chatted off and on, I tried to just follow Brenda's lead. I listened when she felt like talking and tried to help carry the weight of the silence when she retreated and was quiet. We talked about mundane everyday topics like our families, our Valpo friends, shared work frustrations and whether she should be grateful that Hank cleaned the carpets or annoyed that he had left the carpet cleaner out in the living room, unmoved, for the last 2 months. And, interspersed, she would offer random recollections about what had happened.

The conversation moved, without continuity or intelligible transition, back and forth between the mundane and the raw, violent, reality of what had happened. Brenda recounted, as best as she remembered, the events of the evening leading

PART 4: LOVING

up to the attack and rape. She talked about the struggles and roadblocks she and her colleague had been facing during their trip and the complex and corrupt nature of business in Sochi. She talked about the extreme language barrier outside the confines of their hotel, and how, over the course of the week, she and her colleague had found respite in the hotel bar after the long days of thwarted business. And, true to Brenda's nature, she had made friends with perfect strangers on the other side of the world.

She told me about the other business people that were there over the course of the week and that night in particular. Different contractors, from all over the world, all there like Brenda, "on business", in some fashion or another, in advance of the Sochi Olympics. She told me about one guy in particular who had propositioned her, and how she, in her good-natured, no-harm-no-foul, way rebuffed him and continued on with the merriment of her newfound friends. She recounted what she had had to drink — "a shot of vodka, a beer and a half, and a shot of tequila" — noting, with a tone of self-defense, that she wasn't a "lightweight" and that those drinks alone would not have been enough to make her black out, someone must have put something in her drink and drugged her. But who? And how? She didn't know. And those unanswered (and unanswerable) questions came again and again and again. The missing six hours of time, the not knowing who or what or how many, was eating at her and, despite being a lawyer and being in the business of answering the unanswerable questions, I had no answers. All I could do was listen. And console. And reassure.

As Brenda offered up the often-disjointed pieces of her recollection, one theme that emerged was that of self-doubt, self-blame, and shame. Did she drink too much and leave herself vulnerable to this happening? "I'm not a lightweight — you know me, Kim, I can hold my liquor." "Did I ask for this to happen? Is it my fault?" "I'm sure the surveillance tapes from the hotel bar would make me look like a slut — I was drinking, I was flirting." "How I could I *let* this happen?" "I'm 38 years old and ended up getting raped by a guy (or guys?) that I met at a bar."

I could see her brain cycling over and over with these thoughts. I felt confident that I knew what she was thinking because I was thinking the same thing: How could this have happened? She was smart. She was strong. She knew what to do and what not to do. And yet, it did happen. To her. To my friend. I, of course, assured her, repeatedly, that it wasn't her fault and that there was no shame. And I absolutely meant those words. But to say those words with conviction, and as the absolute truth I knew and know them to be, was to implicitly acknowledge that it could happen to anyone, myself included. That being smart and strong, and knowing what to do, sometimes just isn't enough. To say that you have no culpability or fault in causing an event or action is, in effect, to admit that you have no absolute control in stopping that event or action. That's a hard truth to accept, in particular for a Type-A personality like me, who thrives on maintaining order and control. But as unsettling and uncomfortable as acknowledging that truth was, I knew with absolute certainty that this wasn't Brenda's fault and that if I could assure her of only one thing, that had to be it. She was still smart. She was still strong. This was NOT her fault.

We spent most of Sunday in our yoga pants, talking, not talking, just being. Hank and I were both trying to anticipate Brenda's needs without stifling or overwhelming her, trying to identify, and then negotiate that fine line between being helpful and being annoying. At some point in the evening, Brenda decided she wanted an ice cream sandwich from a specific restaurant. Brenda didn't want to leave the house and decided that she would stay back (the kids were home) and take a shower while Hank and I went out to get the requested ice cream. When we left, Brenda was in good spirits, joking about how we had to hurry to get there before the store closed early because it was Sunday.

When we returned, we found Brenda, unshowered, curled up in her bed, crying. I crawled into the bed with her and, again, just tried to be present, let her feel me there, that she was not alone. Through her tears, she told me that she was sad that I was leaving in the morning, but that she knew I had to get back to go to work. And then she started crying inconsolably. To her, at that moment, it felt like everyone was going back to life as usual on Monday morning while she was stuck in this vortex of physical and emotional pain. Hank assured her that he wasn't going anywhere and that he would stay home and be with her for as long as she needed. I, of course, told her that I was always only a phone call away and that I would come back again soon. But the reality was that, although Brenda felt stuck in place, treading water trying to just survive from one moment to the next, the world did keep spinning, and life around her kept moving forward.

As the months and then years passed after the rape, and after Brenda had been diagnosed with PTSD, she went through a litany of prescription drug cocktails to help her sleep (but not too much) and to temper the anxiety (but not so much as to render her incoherent), and various therapy treatments to help her process the emotions and fears (but not so much as to send into a dissociative state and emotional tailspin). The PTSD diagnosis gave a name to what Brenda was suffering, but it offered little in terms of how to move on, get better, go back to being the "before Brenda".

As a result of the PTSD and its debilitating effects, Brenda was forced to accept that she really couldn't return to the job and career that she loved. Not only could she no longer navigate the long commute, either by car in the infamous Chicago traffic or by train with all the congestion and people, but the substantive demands of the job (high-stakes decisions, social interactions, and travel) were all triggers for her PTSD, sending her into anxiety attacks and dissociative states. Eventually, she was placed on long-term disability and was permanently replaced at her job. That was a hard reality to accept. The world really was moving on without her, and she knew it. Not only was she still reeling from aftershocks of the rape and the PTSD, but now she had lost her professional identity.

Brenda and I didn't talk or communicate as regularly as we used to. We talked less, in part, because we no longer had the naturally carved out time of our commutes and because all calls had to be timed to ensure the kids wouldn't be around to overhear since, at the time, they still didn't know what had happened to Brenda. But our communication suffered most because Brenda had retreated into herself and wouldn't emerge for days, sometimes weeks, from her bed other than to go through the motions of meeting the immediate needs of her family. The vast majority of my phone calls and text messages went unanswered. I was grateful for the times that I texted, and I would see the three dots appear, indicative on the iPhone that she was responding. On the occasions that she did respond to my texts, or even more rarely, answered my phone call, we would pick up where we left off — catching up on the everyday mundane topics of life interspersed with discussions of how she was doing, the medication and therapy regimens, and the overwhelming frustration she felt about not being better yet, about feeling like she was making progress and "getting better," only then to suffer a PTSD trigger and find herself back in bed, unshowered, for days on end.

As a friend, watching from the periphery, it seems that's the cruelest thing about PTSD — that by its very nature,

PART 4: LOVING

it keeps systematically robbing Brenda of her confidence in her own strength and progress every time she experiences a setback. From her vantage point, in the thick of the everyday reality of it, every "bad day" and setback effectively erases any progress that she's made because it means she's not back to being the "before Brenda". She views it as an all-or-nothing proposition. She's either "all" better and should be able to go back to the life she had, or she's still broken and damaged and helpless (and maybe even hopeless). I can't help her through this treacherous minefield that is PTSD; it's a path she has to traverse on her own.

Over the last few years, I have tried (and continue to try) to be a lens for her — to show her what the rest of us see in her, even when she can't see it in herself. The progress that she's made and the strength that she has is real and powerful. Although the top of the mountain still feels out of reach, she owes it to herself to acknowledge and celebrate how far she's already climbed.

I can't begin to count the number of times that Brenda has asked me over the years, "when will I just be better, be back to my old self?", back to being the "before Brenda". In the early days, my answer was always, I don't know, but hang in there, you'll get there. My answer now is that "after Brenda" is even stronger and smarter and braver than the "before Brenda". And while "after Brenda" may never again be a high-powered ad executive traveling the globe, she's amazing in her own right and is following her new calling of helping other women struggling with their own before and afters with the writing of this book.

I look forward to someday running that 5k with my dear friend "after Brenda" (well, not really, but I look forward to our post-5k celebration), and to picking up our Valpo girls' weekends. And I know that that day will come because, while the events in Sochi definitely changed her, they don't define her. The light and presence have returned to her eyes, she is driven by new purpose to help people, and every day that mountaintop gets one step closer.

"MY BRENDA"

A MOTHER'S PERSPECTIVE

"My Brenda." I've called her that since the day her mother, my sister, passed away in 1995. At 14 Brenda had lost her dad to a sudden heart attack and then at 20 years old with the death of her mom, she had lost both parents. For me, this precious young woman who had already faced so much heartache and loss would slip into the role of the daughter I had never had. For her, I would become the mother figure she needed at such a young age. We both assumed these roles willingly although I don't really believe she knew what that would entail until she married and had children of her own.

I have loved her, my niece, my Godchild, My Brenda, since the day she was born and every day since. I have always told her "I couldn't love you more if I had birthed you myself!" I refer to her as my Brenda because to refer to her as my daughter would be confusing to people who know I only had one child, a son, but also because she is my sister's daughter. No one can take my sister's place in Brenda's life, and that has never been my goal. I am simply someone who has had the honor of loving her and being loved by her in this lifetime.

When Brenda and her husband Henry were expecting their first child, they surprised my husband and me with an "Honorary Grandparent" Certificate. Their children, my deceased sister's grandchildren, became our grandchildren. No questions asked and never looking back, we proceeded to become Nana and Papa to two beautiful grandchildren long before we ever dreamed possible and with more joy than we ever imagined.

I'd like to think we both hit the jackpot by being able to be there for one another over the years. We have both reaped the joys of a lovingly close relationship without some of the tug-of-war or animosities that can come from a biological mother/daughter history. I think we are freer to love, laugh and say what we think because there are fewer constraints.

I was diagnosed with Breast Cancer in 2002, the year Brenda's first child was born. I went through the treatments and did everything they told me to do, but the cancer came back in my bones in 2008, and I have been battling it ever since. Brenda has always been there to lend a hand when things get tough, and an ear to listen, but in many ways, I have tried to protect her from my terminal prognosis. I realize protecting her from any of this is futile, but as someone who loves her and knows the losses she has had in her life, I still try. She has been very stoic, very matter of fact and down to business, but I realize this is hard for her. I wonder if she cries when she's not with me. I hate that this is one more crummy thing on her plate and I hate that I am the one causing sadness in her life. It sounds silly, but I would give anything if she didn't have to deal with my having cancer!

In September of 2013, Brenda called me and said she needed to come over and talk to me and that she was bringing her best friend, Kelly. My heart was pounding, my head started racing to all the conversations we might be having. Was her marriage in trouble, had she herself been diagnosed

PART 4: LOVING

with some terrible illness, was something wrong with one of the kids? She lives 70 miles away, why was she with Kelly coming to my house?

When Brenda came in the front door, she looked like a shell of herself. Writing this today I can still see her face, and if I'm totally honest here, my first thought was that Henry had hurt her; emotionally and physically. And yet, I could not then and cannot now ever conceive of the idea that Henry would physically harm her. I'm ashamed of those thoughts as I type them now, but for an instant they were real. There were bruises that seemed to be fading so whatever had happened to her had not just happened. She seemed to be exhausted and in shock. I would find out later that it had taken her a week to come and tell me. It was her way of protecting me (we have a pattern of wanting to do that for each other!) and also her way of keeping her distance so she could try to deal with what had happened before she shared it with me and later, her brother. I can only imagine how difficult it must have been for her to actually put together the plan to come and try to put into words the horror of what had happened to her.

There are some things about that day I cannot remember, like who actually said the words "drugged and raped", Brenda or Kelly? I had known she was going to Russia, but what day had she actually come home? My dearest friend in the world came into the picture at some point but had she been there or did she come when she heard Brenda was coming to talk?

What I do remember like it was yesterday is wrapping her up in a gentle hug that I prayed would make it better. All I wanted at that moment was to make it better for her. This couldn't be happening, not to my Brenda, and yet here she was in my Family Room telling me that this horrific crime had happened to her.

I know I cried, I know I was thinking of a million questions, and some of them were tumbling out of my mouth. And then I remember realizing that no matter what had happened to her, all that really mattered was that she **was** here in my Family Room alive! I watch the news, I know that many times the victims of rape never come home. She had been drugged and raped in Russia and still came home to us. What if the person/persons who did this to her had killed her and dumped her body somewhere or sold her into a sex traffic ring? What if she had never come home from Russia and we never knew what happened to her? What if her husband and children spent the rest of their lives searching for her? As horrific as hearing about the rape was, these thoughts were even more unthinkable.

I remember these emotions jumping around in my head as I sat and stared at her, feeling devastated about what had happened, but thanking God that she was alive. I know that she is alive and with her family today because of God's Grace. He has plans for her, and He brought her home to her husband and children because her work here is not done. I think that this book and helping others is part of that work and recovery. Her children who were phenomenal even before this happened to their mother, have flourished with her daily presence in their lives. God's path for her was greater than being a Jane Doe in Russia. Thanks be to God that he has other plans for her and we are reaping the benefits of those plans.

For a while after the rape, Brenda would come and stay with me during the day, so she didn't have to be home alone. I cherished those days she was in my home and feeling loved and safe enough to take naps. Just having her know she wasn't alone was something I could do. I would have given anything to take her pain and suffering away, but as moms we know that's not how it works. We can love them through their

PART 4: LOVING

darkest times, and we can walk with them through some of the fears, but we can never do it for them. We can only cheer them on from the sidelines and cry for them in private.

She would go through stages of not answering calls or texts. I knew I had to call her out on that because as I think I said to her at the time, "loving people and being part of a family means you have a responsibility to let them know how you are, even if it's the briefest, 'I'm OK, I just need some space' response."

And then one day my anger kicked in. The anger was not at her, but at the fact that this had happened to her. As a woman, it makes me angry that we are vulnerable simply because of the way our Creator designed us and men can do things like this to us and destroy the person we were meant to be. Brenda was no longer the person she should have and could have been. How can one human being do that to another? How would we/I ever get her back emotionally and could she ever really come back from this and be whole again? All because some jerk needed to exert his power over a woman for whatever sadistic reason! I was mad as hell, and yet I couldn't share that with her, she needed my words to be soothing and gentle. She was not to blame for this person taking advantage of her because she was a female. My anger was not going to help her in any way, and thankfully I found other healthy outlets for it.

Between the bouts of anger were the moments of sheer terror. Terror that during a conversation she would nonchalantly mention that she had lost several hours and wound up someplace unfamiliar. One time she wound up in a parking lot at O'Hare Airport, and another time in a cemetery in some odd town. Wait, what did she just tell me in our phone conversation and did she realize it would scare the crap out of me, so she tried to pass it off as nothing? Those were the days when I wanted to hear from her all the time, and yet she was pulling away and having these bizarre experiences. I wanted to drive to her home and spend every moment of every day with her. Again, those days were sheer torture and sheer terror for me, I can't imagine what it must have been like living in her head.

Brenda's timeline for returning to work following this nightmare was unrealistic, to say the least. I knew it, anyone who loved her knew it, but she didn't know it. However, one thing I know to be true is that this woman has always had high expectations of herself and so I would have expected nothing less than her goal to return to work quickly. I think it took her by surprise that returning to work might need to be a long-term goal. I knew that this beautiful, vibrant, outgoing, trusting, powerhouse-of-a-woman needed time to weep for herself and to grieve for a new kind of loss. She needed time to hear and digest that none of this was her fault, that she is still a beautiful, vibrant, less trusting, powerhouse woman who just might need to ask for comfort and ice cream one day and to be in the gym working out like a beast the next.

My heart broke for my Brenda in September 2013. It broke for Henry and their children, and it breaks a little more every time I see her struggling with the PTSD and every time I see how much she has grieved over the loss of a career that she worked so hard to build. But my heart soars every time I hear her laugh and see her with her husband and their children. My heart is happy when I see that she is here and alive with all of us who love her. The life she thought she would have was stolen from her in Russia, but we who love her win because we still have her here with us.

Every day is a victory, every time her children have a birthday, or something as simple as a story to share with her is a win because she is here. Every holiday is sweeter because she is here sharing it with all of us. Every Christmas

PART 4: LOVING

Eve since 2013 when our family gathers to celebrate, I have looked at my Brenda and held back tears of what if, what if she had never come home from that trip to Russia and we were still searching for her? How different would every detail of our lives be if she hadn't come back to us? And then I hold back happy tears of joy and thankfulness to God that she is here, sitting in a room with us and watching her children and their cousins open their gifts. She is at the dining room table sharing a meal with all of us and laughing and loving.

While I know that every detail of her life has changed, I pray that she knows how much she is loved and cherished, I pray she can see past some of the pain and loss that this has created in her life and see a future that is happy and filled with love because she is here with all of us who love her so very deeply.

Part 5: Rejoicing

A Survivor's Victory Dance

I am not a victim. No matter what I have been through, I'm still here. I have a history of victory.

–Dr. Steve Maraboli

A Victory Dance

At this point, you have to be wondering — why did I write this book? I don't have the answers. I don't have the "cure." When I started writing, it was to tell my story. To give a voice to all of the women and men who haven't had a chance to tell their stories. To put a face to PTSD and the people who love us.

But as I've typed and recounted and rehashed the horrendous and often depressing details from the past four years of my life, I discovered what my support team has been trying to get me to see for years. I SURVIVED. And if you're reading this, YOU have survived. YOU have survived every single horrible thing that has ever happened to you up until this moment. You are alive, and you are alive for a reason.

If you're in a dangerous situation — get out. If you are leading a lifestyle that puts you in danger — get out. If you are sad or anxious or depressed or stressed, I get it! I know what it's like to not be able to get out of bed or make it through the day without taking a nap. I've gone more than a few days without a shower or brushing my teeth. I know what it's like not to be able to work but worry about how to make ends meet. I know what it's like to be having a perfectly fine day and then have something trigger a panic attack. If you are suffering, I am sorry. I am so, so sorry and I hope you find peace.

Please, if you're not already seeing somebody, seek professional help. I would not have made it this far without my amazing medical team. I had to try a lot of treatment approaches, with a lot of trial and error, to find a combination that works for me — and that's only most of the time. I still have lapses, and, according to the last independent psychologist I saw for a second opinion, I will have ups and downs for the rest of my life.

After writing this, my eyes have been open. My life, even with this crazy thing called PTSD, is an amazing gift. Your life is a gift. You were meant to live it. Listen to the universe. It gives us signs every single day, we just need to pause to see them, to hear them, to be open to them and then to have the courage to follow them.

My career in advertising is over. I spent 17 years building it, and in one night, because of one (?) man, I lost it. I was stripped of the creativity and the comradery. I was stripped of the team that I adored and clients that I respected. I was stripped of my sweet, comfortable salary and my airline miles. I was stripped of my self-esteem and my confidence. I lost my purpose for waking up in the morning. I lost myself.

But in the past four years, I've found a new appreciation for my husband. He has been my rock in ways I never imagined I would need him. While I lost more than a few along the way, I found out who my true friends are. They have a better relationship with my voicemail than me, but they never stop calling, and they ALWAYS pick up when I need them. I had the opportunity to write this book. To find a new kind of creativity. To put words to the feelings that have haunted me for years. I had the chance to really get to know my kids. For better or for worse, I was a stay at home mom during their formative middle school years. Someday, probably soon, they will know my story. They've seen me at my worst, sad and weak, but I'm hoping after they know

PART 5: REJOICING

what I've been through, what I SURVIVED, they will see my strength. This is my story. I am strong. I am a survivor. I am resilient. Nobody can take that away from me, from you, from us. Rock on.

PART 6: KNOWING

KNOWLEDGE IS POWER

*Hope is not pretending that troubles don't exist.
It is the hope that they won't last forever.
That hurts will be healed, and difficulties overcome.
That we will be led out of the darkness
and into the sunshine.*

www.livelifehappy.com

Tips for Traveling Safer

Most people who travel for work consider themselves savvy business travelers. I was one of those people. With more than 500,000 airline miles logged, I was confident that I knew what I was doing. I'd traveled all over the U.S. and had spent weeks at a time in Europe and Asia. It wasn't until I was a victim of a heinous crime overseas that I realized I wasn't taking my personal safety as seriously as I should. Here are some things I wish I knew:

If you can, avoid traveling alone. There's safety in numbers.

If you are traveling with a co-worker, **request to have rooms on the same floor**, preferably near each other. I don't think I would have been taken if I wasn't walking down the hallway by myself.

Text your co-worker (or a loved one if you're traveling alone) to let them know you made it back to your room safely. Lynn had no idea that I'd been taken. She assumed I'd made it back to my room with no problems after I got off the elevator. I was missing for six hours, and she had no clue.

Always make sure a loved one has your itinerary along with emergency contact information for your employer should something happen to you. Henry had my flight and hotel information. He knew I was traveling with Lynn (didn't know her last name or have her phone #). He knew a lot of my co-workers by name but didn't know how to contact any of them or how to reach my boss. Henry knew something was wrong when I wasn't returning his texts for six hours, but he didn't have anyone to call to check on my whereabouts.

If you're traveling internationally, **know the number of the US Embassy**. I didn't know I could call them for help until I returned to the US and the FBI asked me why I hadn't reached out to them. I was hurt and in shock. It never even crossed my mind. Additionally, the **US State Department has a program called STEP – Smart Traveler Enrollment Program** which is a free service that allows U.S. citizens traveling abroad to enroll their trip with the nearest U.S. Embassy or Consulate. You'll receive important information from the Embassy about safety conditions in your destination country. Additionally, it will help the U.S. Embassy contact you in an emergency, whether natural disaster, civil unrest, or family emergency.

Be wary of groups of people as it's easier to fall prey to distraction tactics. While one person is engaging you in conversation, the other person could be slipping something into your drink or robbing you blind. Don't forget, kids can be criminals too. Trust nobody.

Remember the basics you learned in college. Drink to have fun, but keep your wits about you. Use the buddy system. Don't leave your drink unattended. Don't accept drinks from strangers.

Other Useful Tips You May or May Not Know

Always keep a copy of your passport page with somebody at home and another either electronically or hidden somewhere in your luggage. This will give you a starting point with the Embassy in the event your passport is lost/stolen.

Let your financial institution know you'll be traveling abroad.

Don't carry any extra bling that you don't need – this includes jewelry/currency/electronics.

If you're lost, don't stand in the middle of the street looking like a lost tourist. Find a café or someplace more private to gather your bearings.

If you're in a non-English-speaking country, carry a business card for your hotel with you at all times. If you get lost, need to take a cab, etc. you have a way to communicate where you need to go.

Put the Do Not Disturb sign on your door and leave the TV on. This will distract thieves from entering your room while you're out.

Always keep whatever valuables you are leaving in your room in the safe.

Have a plan on who and when you'll be checking in with back home.

Tips for Survivors

(as published on the JoyfulHeartFoundation.org web page)

Deciding to get help is a personal decision that belongs to the survivor alone. A person who has been sexually assaulted has already endured a lot and often the thought of talking to someone or seeking medical attention can be overwhelming. It is important to keep in mind, however, that there are some recommended actions a survivor can take that can be beneficial in the future.

Believe in yourself. Know that when you are forced to have any form of sexual contact without your consent, it is not your fault.

Find a safe environment—anywhere away from the attacker. Contact someone immediately. Go to this person's house or have them go to where you are. Ask someone you trust to stay with you for support.

Seek medical attention immediately. Do not change your clothes, bathe, or brush your teeth. If possible, refrain from using the bathroom. This can help to preserve evidence if you choose to make a police report. Going to the hospital does not mean you have to notify the police. It is for your medical safety to be examined. Even with no visible physical injuries, it is important to determine if internal injuries were sustained (such as tearing or bruising) and to weigh the risks of sexually transmitted diseases and pregnancy.

Preventative medication can be provided if the circumstances are appropriate.

If you are able to, write down all the details you can recall about the assault and the perpetrator. Or ask a friend you can confide in to record this information for you.

Call the National Sexual Assault Hotline, operated by RAINN, for free, confidential counseling, 24 hours a day: 1-800-656-HOPE. When you call, you will be connected to your local rape crisis center. An advocate may be available to meet you at the hospital.

In order to preserve any forensic evidence, ask the nurse, doctor and/or advocate to explain what the forensic rape kit is, how it is performed, what the process is once it is completed and the benefits of the procedure. If there was no penetration, you might still have the kit completed to obtain evidence elsewhere on your body.

If you suspect you may have been drugged, report immediately to hospital staff. The window period to collect evidence of drugs (either through a urine sample or blood) is extremely short. The sample will be analyzed at a forensic lab.

Report the sexual assault to local law enforcement authorities, even if the assault occurred in another district. An advocate can provide the information you'll need to understand the criminal justice system process.

Recognize that healing from sexual assault or any trauma takes time. Allow yourself the time you will need to recover emotionally, mentally, and physically. There is no set time frame for your healing process.

National Resources for Survivors

Rape, Abuse, and Incest National Network
1.800.656.4673
www.rainn.org

National Child Abuse Hotline
1.800.422.4453
www.childhelp.org

National Domestic Violence Hotline
1.800.799.7233
www.ndvh.org

National Teen Dating Abuse Helpline
1.866.331.9474
www.loveisrespect.org

National Suicide Prevention Lifeline
1.800.273.8255
www.suicidepreventionlifeline.org

Acknowledgements

There are so many people to thank for helping me get through the process of writing my first book.

First and foremost, Henry. The world's most patient man and an amazing husband. Thank you for all the coffee and ice cream trips you have made over the course of the past four years. Thank you for not moving out of our bedroom after I punched you in my sleep the first time (or the tenth). Thank you for holding my hand, for loving me through this and never, ever quitting on us. You are the love of my life.

To Kelly, my BFF for life. Thank you for always being patient with me, for crying with me and helping me find the humor in even the darkest of situations. I could not have made it through those first 96 hours without your constant love and support. I could not have made it through the past 30+ years without your friendship. You are my rock. I love you.

To Aunt Susan, the last gift my Mom ever gave me was asking you to love me when she was gone. You have been a constant source of love and light in my life. You have been my mom, my kids' nana, and my friend. Always honest, always caring, always giving, always strong. You are one of the greatest blessings in my life. I love you.

To Kim, the world's greatest college roommate and life-long friend. Thank you for hopping on a plane when I needed you most. For understanding my special kind of crazy. For donuts after workouts. For having a better relationship with my voicemail than me sometimes. For checking in when I go radio silent and for the endless amount of Hallmark cards that have shown up in the mail over the years. You are the best. I'm so grateful to have you in my life.

To my kids, for putting up with my endless hours of naps. For keeping me company in my Zen den while I worked on my book. For cheering me on and believing this book is going to change the world. For all the laughs and for loving each other. You guys are awesome. Being your Mom is the best job in the world.

To my cousin Lynn, for being "my person" through every crisis I've ever had in my lifetime.

To Jason and Amy, for the hugs and the tears and all the beers. I am so lucky to have you as my family.

To Tracy, my first draft editor. Thank you for all the grammar corrections and color-coded notes (especially the purples). You are my cousin by chance, but my sister by heart.

To Kim Rhodes, Suzanne Paroutka and Dr. Shea, thank you for giving me a safe place to heal. For making me feel cared for not just as a patient, but as a person. You all saved my life in so many ways. Thank you.

To everyone who donated to my GoFundMe — I couldn't have gotten this book published without your support. THANK YOU!

To every survivor who opened up and shared their stories with me — you are courageous, and I appreciate you sharing your strength with me. Peace and love to you all.

Epilogue

May 2021. It's been four years since I wrote this book. My plan was to publish it at that time, but due to circumstances beyond my control, I was advised to wait. Last May, I was given the go ahead to finally move forward, but I mentally couldn't do it. I began to second guess myself. Does the world really need to hear my story? It's been seven+ years since I was raped. My intention in writing this book has always been to build awareness around the subject of sexual assault. Does the book really convey this or will people deem this as attention seeking behavior? A lot has changed since I first wrote this, do I need to re-write it?

I sat down today and read the book for the first time in over a year. To change anything in this book would be to invalidate where I was physically, emotionally and spiritually four years ago. My life has evolved, but the truth in my story and my feelings at the time still have meaning. Somebody, somewhere, is in the same place I was when I first put pen to paper. Maybe that person is you.

So where am I today? I still suffer from PTSD but I can say with confidence that I no longer consider it a weakness. It's certainly an inconvenience but I've come to learn that I am far from weak. I've made adjustments in my life to minimize my triggers. When my symptoms flare up, and they still do, I know that I am strong enough to overcome a bad day. My kids are almost grown. Makena left for college and Braeden is going to be a Senior next year. They've both helped friends work through the aftermath of sexual assaults, so I know talking with them was the right choice. As much as I want to shield them from the ugliness in this world, rape happens to 1 in 6 women. Sadly, that number hasn't changed. That is why I wrote this book. Thanks for reading. Thanks for sharing. Be kind always.

NOTES

Besides garnering all of the love and support my friends and family offered, I read more than thirty books that offered inspiration and guidance to me when I was desperately looking for hope. Here is the list of my Top Ten favorite books and their authors. Thank you for sharing your own stories, your words of wisdom and your values. I am a fan and would love to grab coffee sometime (wink-wink).

Big Magic: Creative Living Beyond Fear by Elizabeth Gilbert

The Deeper Path: Five Steps That Let Your Hurts Lead to Your Healing by Kary Oberbrunner

Everything Happens for a Reason: Finding the True Meaning of the Events in Our Lives by Mira Kirshenbaum

The Four Agreements: A Practical Guide to Personal Freedom by Don Miguel Ruiz

Furiously Happy: A Funny Book About Horrible Things by Jenny Lawson

Lucky by Alice Sebold

Rising Strong: The Reckoning. The Rumble. The Revolution by Brene Brown

The Universe Has Your Back: Transform Fear to Faith by Gabrielle Bernstein

Whole: How I Learned to Fill the Fragments of My Life with Forgiveness, Hope, Strength, and Creativity by Melissa Moore and Michele Matrisciani

You Are a Badass: How to Stop Doubting Your Greatness and Start Living an Awesome Life by Jen Sincero

BRING BRENDA INTO YOUR ORGANIZATION

Brenda is an author, certified coach, speaker, trainer and rape advocate. She speaks on topics related to overcoming life's obstacles by learning to navigate the roadmap to resilience. She is willing to share her story or snippets that are most relevant to you or your group including, but not limited to: the challenges of working motherhood, corporate travel safety, rape, PTSD support, or the role spirituality has played in her recovery. With nearly 20 years in the advertising industry, she is a poised professional ready to speak to any group of any size.

Contact Brenda today to begin the conversation:
BrendaGAuthor@gmail.com

www.ingramcontent.com/pod-product-compliance
Lightning Source LLC
LaVergne TN
LVHW011821060526
838200LV00053B/3855